The Many Faces *of*
JOURNALING

Topics & Techniques for
Personal Journal Writing

by
Linda C. Senn

The Many Faces *of*
JOURNALING

Topics & Techniques for Personal Journal Writing

Second Edition
Completely Revised

by
Linda C. Senn

PEN
CENTRAL
PRESS

St. Louis, Missouri

Other books by Linda C. Senn:

The Many Faces of Journaling, 1st ed.
And Now We Dance: Journaling for the Woman Within
Your Pocket Divorce Guide
The Divorce Recovery Journal (co-authored with Mary Stuart, M.A.)
The Basic Divorce Workbook
10 Effective Ways to Promote Your Seminar

Published by:

PEN CENTRAL PRESS
Division of Pen Central Communications
P. O. Box 220369
St. Louis MO 63122-0369

Thanks to Ghost Junction Band for permission to use lyrics of "Selfish Song."

ATTENTION Schools & Organizations: Quantity discounts available on order of this book for educational purposes or fund raising. Contact Pen Central Press, address above, ph. 314-984-9805, fx 314-821-8482, email info@PenCentralOnline.com

Publisher's Cataloging-in-Publication
(Provided by Quality Books, Inc.)

Senn, Linda C.
    The many faces of journaling : topics & techniques for personal journal writing / by Linda C. Senn. -- 2nd ed.
    p. cm.
    Includes bibliographical references and index.
    ISBN-13: 978-0-9665672-9-8
    ISBN-10: 0-9665672-9-3

    1. Diaries--Authorship. 2. Diaries--Authorship-- Psychological aspects. 3. Creative writing.
    4. Self-actualization (Psychology)   I. Title.

PN4390.S46 2008   808'.02
                        QBI08-600119

Author's Preface

Of the many benefits of personal journaling, two lead the parade: coping with today and creating a legacy for tomorrow. One aspect may be more compelling than the other for you at the moment, but chances are you'll shift back and forth honoring both the now and the years to come.

Old journals are amazing portals to the past. I've kept journals in one form or another for most of my life, and reading back over them reintroduces me to the many changes that have occurred in my life over that time.

In revisiting my adult journals, I find that some entries stir a sense of pride in how I handled a difficult situation or reawakened my dormant backbone. Others remind me of pain that I hope never ever to experience again. Still others bring back fresh surges of joy and laughter. How amazing! All the people in those many journals are me!

Sharing my journaled dreams with my therapist proved enlightening, yielding either small insights or startling revelations about past pain. The same therapist, Dr. Pamela Nickels, often sent me home to write out the smoldering rage I was trying so valiantly to ignore. And when we wanted to invite the Linda-child of long ago into the counseling process, Pam suggested I write with crayons.

The tools of journaling will be different for different people, and for the same person in varying moods—pen, pencil, markers, or computer keyboard and plain or fancy paper. I've written with such fury that my pen gouged through the next few pages. I've pounded the computer keyboard in the wee hours, "shouting" in 72-point bold-faced type, hammering out all kinds of venomous language. (*God bless password-protected files!*) It felt good and it helped. It's hard to let go of our rage until we allow ourselves to acknowledge it. Alternately, I've written a great many lyrical, bubbly entries when joy filled my heart to overflowing.

The journaler isn't the only one helped by this kind of writing. Our journals can also benefit those dear to us. Children love to know that someone is writing about them, recording their accomplishments and clever repartee. We have so much to share with our young people— stories that can give them a greater sense of family and self, of history and of the simple insights of daily observation.

And remember—there's no wrong way to journal. It's intimately and joyfully your show from start to … well, journals are rarely finished, are they? Even a travel journal remains a work in progress as you recall details and insights that eluded you during the initial writing.

Observe, ponder, write, and enjoy!

Linda Senn
January 2001

This second edition of *The Many Faces of Journaling* includes two new chapters. The Scrapbook Journaling chapter offers guidelines for creating written entries on scrapbook pages to add flavor and depth of information to the visual joy of the photos.

The Environmental Journaling chapter addresses earth-friendly journaling and shows how to create your own written "platform" for evaluating the news reports, scientific findings, and actions (or inactions) of the world population on environmental change and global warming. Recording your thoughts can help you analyze your own take on the subject and will provide a record for future generations to learn from.

Linda Senn
March 2008

Acknowledgments

My deepest thanks go to Heather Tisdel and Vera Glick for their skilled, editorial work on this book and their unflagging encouragement and enthusiasm. I'm also enormously grateful to Cheryl Abbott, David Breeden (Dr. Poetry), and Caitlin Tisdel for their kind and caring support throughout the writing process.

Any book on writing seems to benefit from the use of examples. This one follows that premise. The sample entries throughout the book have been reproduced as submitted without editing. The ages of contributors at the times of their journaling range from 15 to 65+ years of age. They're male and female and come from various walks of life.

Contributions from the following people have greatly enhanced the suggestions offered in this book: Heather E. Tisdel, Kevin T. Tisdel, Cathleen Castillo, Beverly J. Letchworth, Vera Glick, Mary Stuart, Mindy Gramling-Bailey, and to Matt Carlock and the Ghost Junction band.

Because of the intimate and/or revealing nature of their entries, several other people chose to remain anonymous or to use fictitious names.

Note: Entries that show no attribution were written by the author.

The Many Faces of Journaling

Table of Contents

The Many Faces of Journaling

Introduction

Personal journaling can add amazing depth and richness to our lives, both through the actual act of writing and the resultant recorded information. As we begin to keep one or more journals, we gradually discover that we're becoming more keenly aware of the world around and within us.

Most of us enter personal diary- or journal-keeping by way of the standard chronological set-up, one day at a time, writing neatly forward throughout the year, never thinking beyond the confines of the calendar. But that method is about as representative of journaling as Charlie Brown is of the whole Peanuts gang—it's an important face, but only one of many. In *The Many Faces of Journaling,* you'll meet lots of the others.

Throughout the **history of journaling**, writers have worn the faces of youth through old age. Anne Frank wrote as a young teenager, May Sarton as an octogenarian. All left insights and memories unique to their age and experience at the time. Today's children often get their first taste of journaling in kindergarten.

The **personal growth and goals** journal lifts its face to the sunshine in happy anticipation. Here you can make grand plans, build magical castles in the air, and develop practical plans for a career change, all with a sense of truth and honor to your inner hopes. A growth journal usually isn't written for others to read, so it provides a safe place for you to dream your grandest dreams—both the practical and the wistful.

Counselors often encourage their clients to keep a **therapeutic journal** to help process the pain and healing of life crises. This method wears a healer's face. It's an enormously effective way of ventilating anger and making some kind of sense out of past wounds and currently confusing relationships. Journaling is a powerful tool for understanding the inner world of the subconscious and the quietly conscious, enabling us to explore the fascinating, often-stifled world within.

You'll certainly want to include the cheerful, impish grin of an **upbeat journal**! These become the repositories of your excellent accomplishments both grand and small, funny one-liners from various sources, and bits and pieces of whimsy that cross your path. The very act of keeping an upbeat journal helps you become more keenly attuned to the humor around you.

Scrapbooking has become a highly creative, loving art form, featuring visual goodies on every page. But to the face of the artiste, you will overlay one of the scribe. The chapter on **scrapbook journaling** shows how to write accompanying entries to add rich sensory details, event information, and personal notes to the pages in various lengths, styles and arrangements to compliment the photos in the books.

Do you enjoy word play or perhaps want to explore and expand your writing abilities? A **creativity journal** will stimulate your writing talents and show you how to use words as playthings. In time it will become a repository for your original and extraordinarily nifty ideas.

When **journaling for the next generation**, you'll wear the face of a storyteller. This is the perfect place to relate corny family stories and tell how horribly Uncle Whatsis used to tease you when you were kids growing up together. Future generations—scholars, genealogists, and family members—will bless your written recital of family anecdotes, "olden days" experiences, and (for family) their own entry into your world. Be sure to check *Appendix A* for tips on writing fascinating family memoirs.

Have you ever wanted to rewrite history and tell your version of what happened? Enter the **historic perspective journal**. Writing about current (and past) events from your point of view provides real-life physical and emotional settings for historic events. Don your probing reporter's face and write about where you were and how you really felt when President Kennedy was shot or the U. S. bombed Baghdad. This kind of journal can include economic data as well as a down-to-earth look at your home, community, and assorted international facts of the moment. This is your chance to analyze the meanings and possible societal shifts that may ensue from the major events of the day.

One area of current history that provides weekly, if not daily, fodder for reflection is the health of our planet. The **environmental journaling** chapter encourages you to create a written account of this vast, ongoing challenge. Record your own observations, the news of global responses to climate change, the economic and (in)convenience factors, and your evaluation of the reality and immediacy of the problem. Are you a doubter or a crusader? Chances are virtually100% that it will be a journal-without-end.

As the faces of Nature can range all the way from idyllic to deadly, so will the tone of your **nature & gardening journal** entries. Yet you will feel more grounded and at one with the Earth as you journal your observations and develop a deep appreciation of Nature and her steady rhythms in your everyday life. For variety, you might like to include occasional international weather events, such as Hurricane Katrina.

As we record our impressions of Nature, we begin to actually see and hear more than we did before. Then as we search for fresh material for journal entries, we really see instead of merely glancing at her marvels.

The Many Faces of Journaling

For your **dream journaling**, envision the explorer's face, for you'll continually discover new insights into unspoken and scarcely conscious passions and fears. One entry might smack of the superhero curing world hunger, while the next may reveal the deeper message behind what had seemed to be a nonsense dream. Our dreams offer significant images, metaphors, and symbolism through which we may come to better understand ourselves and our relationships with others.

The tried-and-true **chronological journal** still feels homier and more comfortable to some people than more topically specific journals do. Or perhaps that style will simply be the cornerstone of your journal library, with other volumes set up for travel, dreams, gardening, and so forth. Because of the relatively large volume of information recorded in this kind of diary, you'll want to be sure to leave a few blank pages at the front or back of the journal to use as an index of important entries. (*You can't believe how useful it is to be able to check your index for the date of Johnny's last tetanus shot!*)

Your **travel journals** may have the look and feel of a leather-and-pine dude ranch trip; the fleur-de-lis of a wine country sojourn; or the soft, familial comfort of a trip back home. A later rereading of these diaries will instantly transport you back to the joys and excitement of your trips, all to be relived at your leisure.

Somehow each idea, dream, event, and person assumes greater value once we begin our active journaling. In some mysterious way, writing about them makes them more our own than just living through them ever does. As we write, we become life chroniclers and word artists.

As you enter fully into this wonderfully diverse world of journaling, forget about grammar, punctuation, sentence structure, and other rigid dictates. Relax. *Journal from the heart.* Don't force your journaling into a set, daily schedule unless that really is the most comfortable style for you. *Keep it fun.* Expand and deepen the way you record your observations of the world, and your life in particular, in whatever way best suits your temperament and lifestyle.

As you go along, you may discover additional topics that appeal to you. For instance, how about a new recipe journal? Or one based on a new hobby like weaving or woodcarving? Do you enjoy sketching or painting? A journal entry on the back of a work of art can tell the story of how you happened to choose that subject. Experiment.

Reading back over these entries of our life-in-words provides incomparable insights into where we've come from, what we've thought, dreamed, and agonized over, and how we've dealt with both the pleasures and the pains. Time can cloud the memory, but not the written word.

Think about which topics you want to include in each journal and which others might deserve volumes of their own. Journaling for the Next Generation usually works well with Historic Perspective and Environmental Journaling, although I wouldn't try to include any other topics in that book. Likewise, Personal Growth, Dreams, Therapeutic, and Upbeat kinds of journaling tend to complement each other. Creative and Scrapbook Journaling are comfortable companions. Thumb through the Table of Contents and let your brain play with the various combinations.

Notebooks appropriate for journaling range from the spiral-bound, lined notebooks that go on sale at the start of the school year to the fine leather-bound journals in book, travel, and stationery stores. Plan to have a variety of writing tools on hand to suit your mood and topic. Pens of all kinds and colors, pencils, sketching pencils, crayons, highlighters, and markers add zip to your entries and literally bring color to the past.

Through the written word, you can offer the same kind of family stories and wisdom as the tribes of old did around their campfires. You'll be creating a unique legacy.

Through personal journaling, we can honor what was, what is, and what is yet to be. Happy journaling!

Note: Entries that show no attribution were written by the author.

Chapter 1

Journaling Throughout History

*It is delightful to transport one's self
into the spirit of the past,
to see how a wise man has thought before us,
and to what a glorious height
we have at last reached.*

— *Johann Wolfgang von Goethe*

Diaries and journals have been with us since man first recorded the thrill of the hunt on his cave walls. Since that time, we've continued to record our newfound knowledge and achievements in one form or another throughout history. Stone tablets, papyruses, hides, paper, and now computers all have served journalers' purposes.

The excerpts that follow show the original spellings, usages, and abbreviations, which add an extra taste of history in and of themselves. In fact, none of the sample journal entries in this book have been corrected in any way.

The Many Faces of Journaling

Samuel Pepys

The first published diarist of modern times (relative to the cave crew, that is) was 17th century scribe Samuel Pepys (1633 – 1703). Between 1660 and 1669 he wrote an eleven-volume diary or journal that subsequently was published in 1825 long after his death.

Born over his father's tailor shop in London, Pepys's writings provide us with vivid word pictures of life in those times. Here's one of his entries:

January 10, 1664

All our discourse tonight was about Mr Tryan's late being robbed and that Collonell Turner (a mad, swearing, confident fellow, well known by all and by me), one much endebted to this man for his very lifelihood, was the man that either did or plotted it; and the money and things are found in his hand and he and his wife are in Newgate for it - of which we are all glad, so very a known rogue he was.

[When about to be hanged, and engaged in his confession, he put swearing as the first and foremost of his sins. He is said to have had 28 children, counting only those born in wedlock.]

(~ Samuel Pepys)

The Lewis and Clark Expedition

The journals of Captains Meriwether Lewis (1774 – 1809) and William Clark (1770 – 1838); Sergeants Charles Floyd, Patrick Gass, and John Ordway; and Private Joseph Whitehouse tell of their daring expedition from March 3, 1804, to September 26 1806.

December 07, 1804

...the Big-white head chief, of the first village of the Mandans, came to our garrison and told us that the buffaloe were in the prairie coming into the bottom. Captain Lewis and eleven more of us went out immediately, and saw the prairie covered with buffaloe and the Indians on horseback killing them. They killed 30 or 40 and we killed eleven of them. They shoot them with bows and arrows, and have their horses so trained that they will advance very near and suddenly wheel and fly off in case the wounded buffaloe attempt an attack.   (~ Patrick Gass)

December 08, 1804

the Thermometer Stood at 12 d below 0 which is 42 d below the freesing point,...this day being Cold Several men returned a little frost bit, one of [the] men with his feet badly frost bit my Servents feet also frosted & his P--------s a little, I felt a little fatigued haveing run after the Buffalow all day in Snow many Places 18 inches Deep, generally 6 or 8, two men hurt their hips verry much in Slipping down.

(~ William Clark)

James Swan

In the 19th century, pioneer James Swan kept an extensive journal on Native American whaling practices:

Mid-1800s

Scarcely have the (whales) quitted their southern homes before they are surprised by the Indians about the Strait of Juan de Fuca...(who) glide in canoes from island, bluff or bay, rushing upon their prey with whoop and yell, launching their instruments of torture.

The capture having been effected, trains of canoes tow the prize to shore in triumph. The whalemen among the Indians...

are those who delight in the height of adventure and who are ambitious of acquiring the greatest reputation among their fellows.

Eight men make the crew, each wielding a paddle 5 1/2 feet long. The whaling gear consists of harpoons, lines, lances and seal-skin buoys, all of their own workmanship.

(~ James Swan)

Walt Whitman

Walt Whitman (1819 – 1892), who wrote *Leave of Grass* (1900) and other remarkable free verse poetry, also journaled regularly. Some of his entries reflect the importance of diaries and letters during his Civil War experiences.

February 1863

When eligible, I encourage the men [soldiers] to write, and myself, when called upon, write all sorts of letters for them, (including love letters, very tender ones.) Almost as I reel off these memoranda, I write for a new patient to his wife.

(~ Walt Whitman)

May 1864

The men like to have a pencil, and something to write in. I have given them cheap pocket-diaries, and almanacs for 1864, interleav'd with blank paper. (~ Walt Whitman)

Ralph Waldo Emerson

Journaling about friends and activities can be of special interest centuries later, especially if the friend becomes famous. During approximately the same period, Ralph Waldo Emerson (1808 – 1882) wrote of his friend Henry David Thoreau:

March 1856 (age 52)

Yesterday to the Sawmill Brook with Henry. He was in search of yellow violet (pubescens) and menyanthes which he waded into the water for; and which he concluded, on examination, had been out five days. Having found his flowers, he drew out of his breast pocket his diary and read the names of all the plants that should bloom this day, May 20…He thinks he could tell by the flowers what day of the month it is, within two days.

(~ Ralph Waldo Emerson)

Fanny Kemble

Later in that century, Fanny Kemble (1809 – 1893), a famous actress of both British and American stages, was invited to attend the opening of the Liverpool and Manchester Railway, and journaled this reaction to her train ride:

1800s

The most intense curiosity and excitement prevailed, and though the weather was uncertain, enormous masses of densely packed people lined the road, shouting and waving hats and handkerchiefs as we flew by them. We travelled at 35 miles an hour (swifter than a bird flies). When I closed my eyes this sensation of flying was quite delightful.

(~ Fanny Kemble)

Anaïs Nin

Three 20th century diarists stand out from the multitudes of others. French-born writer Anaïs Nin (1903 – 1977) was quite a prolific journalist. Here's an introspective excerpt from one of her journals:

1930s

Am I, at bottom, that fervent little Spanish Catholic child who chastised herself for loving toys, who forbade herself the enjoyment of sweet foods, who practiced silence, who humiliated her pride, who adored symbols, statues, burning candles, incense, the caress of nuns, organ music, for whom Communion was a great event? I was so exalted by the idea of eating Jesus's flesh and drinking His blood that I couldn't swallow the host well, and I dreaded harming ...it.

... At the ages of nine, ten, eleven, I believe I approximated sainthood. And then, at sixteen, resentful of controls, disillusioned with a God who had not granted my prayers (the return of my father), who performed no miracles, who left me fatherless in a strange country, I rejected all Catholicism with exaggeration. Goodness, virtue, charity, submission, stifled me.   (~Anaïs Nin)

Virginia Woolf

Well-born British novelist and essayist Virginia Woolf (1882 – 1941) was a part of the privileged intelligentsia of British society. Her journals reveal a creative and thoroughly outspoken woman. But even this famous diarist neglected her journal from time to time.

November 15, 1921

Really, really—this is disgraceful—15 days of November spent & my diary none the wiser. But when nothing is written one may safely suppose that I have been stitching books; or we have had tea at 4 & I have taken my walk afterwards, or I have had to read something for next days writing, or I have been out late, & come home with stencilling materials, & sat down in excitement to try one.   (~ Virginia Woolf)

The following entry illustrates both the general cultural climate and her specific appraisal of an acquaintance. Notice the sparse but significant detail:

July 22, 1923

A great many conversations to record: dined with Mortimer & Schofield Thayer the other night & went on with them to Mary's.

Mortimer is Oxford, & thus not nearly so easy to come to terms with as Sebastian [Sprott] for instance. He is all angle & polish. Wears a swallow tail white waistcoat; wants brilliancy not intimacy, is half a dandy.   (~ Virginia Woolf)

Anne Frank

Another famed chronicler was Anne Frank, who wrote *The Diary of a Young Girl* between 1942 and 1944 while she and her family were in Amsterdam hiding from the Nazis. Rarely will we find a more poignant collection of personal journal entries than hers.

She received the new diary from her parents on June 14, 1942 for her thirteenth birthday. Twenty-five days later, her family went into hiding in the upper floor of her father's office building to avoid imprisonment. What a change for a young girl just blossoming into womanhood!

July 8, 1942

(the day before the Frank family went into hiding)
Margot [her sister] and I started packing our most important belongings into a schoolbag. The first thing I stuck in was this diary, then curlers, handkerchiefs, schoolbooks, a comb and some old letters. Preoccupied by the thought of going

into hiding, I struck the craziest things in the bag, but I'm not sorry. (~ Anne Frank)

One of the many challenges of avoiding discovery was disposing of the family's refuse:

May 18, 1943

...Although it's undeniably hot, we have to light a fire every other day to burn our vegetable peelings and garbage. We can't throw anything into the trash cans, because the warehouse employees might see it. One small act of carelessness and we're done for! (~ Anne Frank)

And through the bombing and air raid sirens, she navigated adolescence. She was three months shy of her fifteenth birthday when she wrote:

March 17, 1044

...There's something else that displeases them [her parents]: I no longer feel like giving them little kisses morning, noon and night. All those cute nicknames seem so affected, and Father's fondness for talking about farting and going to the bathroom is disgusting. (~ Anne Frank)

On August 4, 1944, Anne and her family were discovered and captured by the Nazis. She died of typhus a few months later at the Bergen-Belsen concentration camp.

So you see, from that first cave wall journaler right on through to the 21st century, people have chosen to record their insights, achievements, experiences, impressions, and opinions either for their own benefit or for the enlightenment of others.

The Many Faces of Journaling

It's a time-honored practice, which has expanded over the centuries to include many aspects that would never have occurred to the early diarists. At least we assume they didn't.

Today's journals can cover virtually all areas of our lives, including playful creativity and the healing of the mind. No longer the primary preserve of the elite or those in authority, journaling is taught in elementary schools and senior centers. We all have valuable information to record. In generations to come, perhaps someone will read our words, and know what life was like for us in the early 21st century.

They'll be intrigued that we had many of the same joys and worries that they experience many years hence, and they'll marvel at our dreams. After all, wouldn't an ancient dream journal make for fascinating reading today?

∝ৣৡ∝

The Many Faces of Journaling

Chapter 2

Personal Growth & Goals Journaling

The most fatal illusion is the settled point of view.
Life is growth and motion;
a fixed point of view kills anybody who has one.

— Brooks Atkinson

To stagnate is to die a little bit each day. We need to aspire to something greater for tomorrow than we know or have today, in order to fully live and enjoy life. And we can augment that growth process immeasurably by recording both the journeys and the achievements.

We grow either through chance or deliberate action. Sometimes personal development sneaks up on us, expanding our horizons while we are off doing other things. Maybe we meet someone new who introduces us to entirely new ways of thinking, or we experience some personal epiphany—an "aha!" moment, when we finally see clearly what had previously been confusing. Recording such insights and expanding upon them in a journal can lead to amazing growth. Some of life's great joys are random, surprise bits of enlightenment.

Many of us fare best when we have specific goals in mind. Those goals may be vague or concrete, long range or immediate, material or ethereal, and they may be revisited and revised frequently. It doesn't matter if we change focus. Personal goals are nobody else's business, so we have no one to answer to when we decide to change course. There's something enormously effective about recording these in a journal. It gives them more prestige, a place of honor, and a firm identity. We tend to take our dreams more seriously when we see them in black and white.

In your Growth Journal, or the growth portion of your larger journal, keep track of both spontaneous and planned times of personal development.

Declared Goals

First declare your goals to yourself in writing, then record your forward progress. Ross Byron wisely wrote, "Few can define their goal, much less write it." Don't wait until the dream is crystal clear. Start ruminating on paper when the ideas first pop into your mind. "Wouldn't it be interesting if…" or "I wonder what it would feel like to…" are both terrific ways to brainstorm and daydream with a pen or keyboard.

Some people routinely make a list of goals every New Year's Day, but that's a matter of personal preference. There's nothing to prevent you from creating or revising your list whenever the mood strikes you.

If you start a fresh journal at the beginning of each year, it's a simple matter to list your goals on page one. (But be sure to leave a few blank pages either at the front or the back of every journal so you can index particularly noteworthy entries.) This was one such entry:

Almost 1992

With just 5 hours of 1991 left, I sit here in my living room "nest" pondering my goals. My accomplishment record isn't always terrific, but I like having goals to shoot for over the course of the year. So here goes –

1 – I'll sell an average of one article a month – minimum! I'm really primed to try the travel writing.
2 – I'll renew 2 fine friendships – Joan and Linda.
3 – I will finally learn to meditate!
4 – I'll test 50 more turn-of-the-century recipes from Grandma's old cookbook.
5 – I'll write my will just to get it out of the way.
6 – I'll spend more time outside – some time every day unless it's raining HARD!

Deborah Weltman, owner of Terra Art and Frame Shop in St. Louis, always includes home and business goals in addition to personal ones. Here are excerpts from her year-2000 goal lists:

Debbie

Business
- hire a display/window person within 1-1½ months
- keep pushing to get rid of [abandoned] gray garage
- get new sign/awning
- paint bathroom
- get semi-regular day off for me!
- try to find more productive use for new section (i.e. 2nd framing area)
- etc......

Home
- plant raised vegetable garden
- remove oak or pine tree from side yard
- add to rock/herb garden
- get new hose holder
- re-do front brick patio
- plant 4 o'clocks under bathroom window
- etc......

Purchases
car
- new car radio
- tune-up
house
- central air conditioner/new furnace
- repair all storm windows/screens
- paint insides of windows
- etc.....

Personal
- more fun time with J.T. [her son]
- more time with friends
- take classes for fun! yoga, gardening ....
- eat less sugar
- visit Anna! [her daughter]
- etc.......   (~ Deborah Weltman)

It's also fun to reread entries written a year or five years ago and compare them to the current situation. Did the goals change direction several times but result in something equally wonderful? Are they still waiting in the wings for their turn? Or have they been replaced with newer dreams? New Year's is also a natural time to contemplate life past and future. Here's an excellent salute to the old year.

The Many Faces of Journaling

New Year's Eve

December 31, 1998 – 8:33 pm...It never ceases to amaze me that one year can carry a life so far...What have I learned this year? Oh, to muse on that would fill the rest of this book. I can outlive heartache and do so with clarity and style, I am good company for myself, I can make it on my own, I like Star Trek and metaphysical poetry and most importantly I learned much about my capacity to believe and live with conviction. Priceless, I know.

The closing of each year is like a tragic death for me. It strikes only the slightest sense of jubilation in what the year to come is—simply put, pure possibility. As I say goodbye to 1998 tonight I know that it will never come again or experience life, it will just break up and float away, adding another wrinkle to our worn faces or layer of pollution to our atmosphere. And 1999 will bring the same along with strange numbers and countless other things that I can scarcely bear to speculate upon.

This year will bring me out of my teens, I will be twenty. I have mixed feeling about this. I almost don't want to let go of all the pain and self-discovery 1998 brought me and yet I half smile at letting it step aside. I am half overjoyed at what might come of all this blankness in front of me. I feel I am finding good enough within myself to fill it well...I guess I should say good-bye to you my friend, your days and hours have taught me much in the time we had and now all that is left is watching the clock until time winds down to the dropping of your funeral ball. I shall think of you often.

(~ Mindy Gramling-Bailey)

Spontaneous Growth

Developing and writing about our personal insights can help us identify our goals and passions in life.

(No date)

Create your world
  as a sanctuary
    with higher purpose,
      order,
        kindness,
          love.

Life is too short
  to wait for the world
    to become what you want it to be.

(~ heather)

Ignoring negative input from others is a major life challenge for many of us. The following entry shows this writer's coming to terms with the disapproval of others.

Sept. 1, 1990

...I'm learning to set boundaries between others' weaknesses and faults and their effect on me. If they're critical, that's their problem. If they're judgmental, that's their problem too. Negatively motivated judgment means nothing to me. I want to work out how to deal with people like this because I can't run away from them all my life.

(~ heather)

Establishing and understanding our personal identity and our place in the scheme of life—past, present, and future—is an ongoing quest. The questions can run the gamut from *Who am I today?* to *What is my place and purpose in the Universe?*

We pray, read, study, and meditate in an effort to make sense of our lives, and frequently learn much in the process. We discuss such things with like-minded people and together come up with new insights. In addition, we may journal about the ongoing quest. The entries usually are a combination of questions and evaluations, with occasional welcome revelations along the way.

One such personal discovery emerged as a result of studying and embracing the theory of reincarnation combined with a recognition of the intricately interwoven threads of family history.

I Am

I just celebrated my Mother's birthday. She's been gone for over 26 years, but I wasn't able to forgive and set aside the pain of my childhood until a week and a half ago. Finally! So while I've never even noticed her birth anniversary in the last many years, it seemed right this year to honor her and thank her for the lessons she taught me.

And as I meditated/prayed/thought about Mom, I realized— I am the product of all the [family] people who have come before me and of all the people I have been before this life. All are a part of who I am today and whatever it is that I'm supposed to do with my tomorrows.

That sounds so simplistic, but in a funny way it makes me feel like I have a whole lot of history and experience buried in me—valuable stuff I can draw upon when I need to. It's like being a spiritual and emotional reservoir and it makes me feel stronger!

During the early months of my divorce recovery period, I ran across *Transitions*, by William Bridges (1980) —a wise book that points out the harm that can result from our tendency to rush from one phase of life to the next without processing the "endings."

In the course of taking time out to heal, I wrote the following poem:

A Time Out

I shall let my soul lie fallow,
   ignore the hassles,
      set aside the multitude of stultifying shoulds,
        and
          simply
            be.

Spiritual Enrichment

From time to time we come across words of wisdom that we particularly want to remember and incorporate into our lives in some way. Include these in your Personal Growth Journal pages.

This Ojibwa Indian prayer is quite beautiful and offers a special message to all those who are involved in creative works.

Ojibwa Indian Prayer

Blessed be the musicians of the world who sing out the song that fills my heart.

Blessed be the painters of the world who capture the forms and colors dancing behind my eyelids.

Blessed be the poets of the world who take the plain words from my lips and hurl them with their magic like scared birds into the sky.

Blessed be the guardians of the legends and dreams for their music and words of love swell within my soul so that we may offer them like a prayer.

Be prepared to take notes during sermons and lectures. They often contain words to live by. During a sermon at our Unitarian church, Reverend John Robinson stated that real personal growth starts beyond the edges of the familiar. I later came across a similar phrase in my reading:

> "...life begins at the end of your comfort level."
> (~ Neale Donald Walsch, *Friendship with God*, 1999)

This directive from the same book is one to incorporate into everyday living:

> "Release the joy that is inside of another, and you release the joy that is inside of you."

Random Openings

Other opportunities for growth fall between the deliberately planned and the purely spontaneous. With delightful frequency they seem to fall into the realm of doors that are opened to us unbidden. Sometimes we've been drifting in that general direction, as in spiritual exploration or career shifts. Other opportunities may seem to be surprises, but on closer inspection stem from some long-held wish or interest.

In some closed-off corner of her mind, a company's newsletter editor may wish she could someday write and publish a non-fiction book. Since she has no topic, publisher, or powerful inspiration going for her, it's scarcely even a daydream.

But at some point in her life synchronicity may kick in, providing both the passion and the means for turning a special topic into a book for public consumption. She wouldn't have listed such a wish as a goal in her journal, but it wasn't purely spontaneous either.

Spiritual growth often falls into that in-between ground. Such was the case when a friend was first introduced to Reiki. Our friend Gwen, who had taken some Reiki training, invited her to attend an open gathering to learn more about this type of healing touch. My friend's life at that time was hectic, and quiet evenings were few and far between. So with a gentle thank you, she let the opportunity pass without another thought.

Months later a professional colleague, Jeanne, happened to mention that she, too, was a Reiki practitioner, and suggested that the friend take Gwen up on her invitation. Since that came from someone who didn't even know Gwen, the friend decided to visit the next gathering. This entry describes her first encounter:

My First Experience with Reiki

My first Reiki Sharing Circle! In the meditation time, I felt a warmth in my hands and in some way understood that it was OK for me to want to excel in this and be special. [My competitive spirit just can't stay out of it!] But that everybody wants that. And I am special, just as everybody is special. My natural drive to really excel at everything I do simply dropped away! And I didn't feel inclined to speak up during the sharing time afterwards, which is unusual for me. I always want to be the helpful little facilitator who keeps the group dialogue going.

When we got the massage tables out and I received the Reiki healing touch [shared a table with John, Jim, and Julie all of whom were new to me], I felt an absolutely incredible sense of peace way down inside. It put me deep into pure feeling beyond words and worry, to a place inside me where I've only been very briefly before, and that was during therapy.

We visitors were invited to participate in "giving" after we'd "received" if we wanted to. I did want to try the "giving," and John guided me so I didn't feel too awkward. Also I saw that almost everybody had their eyes closed in meditation when they were doing the hands-on, so nobody was watching me anyway. What an experience! What a gloriously peaceful place inside of me! I want to get to know that place much, much better.

(~ a Reiki Master)

Spiritual awakening and renewal often comes in its own time, regardless of what other things are going on in our lives. Keeping a record of those first impressions provides a reference point for whatever subsequent steps we choose to take. Those things can so easily be forgotten in the flurry of work, family, shopping, and scrubbing the birdbath. Recording the process of personal development establishes a solid foundation upon which to build and from which to make future evaluations.

Active journaling will often reveal great insights and lead the way to more extensive personal growth than we realize at the ordinary conscious level.

My friend soon decided to take the first Reiki training class simply because she wanted to learn more. A later entry in her journal exemplifies both the joy and confusion of this new interest.

Why Am I learning Reiki?

OK, I didn't know when I visited the Reiki group for the first time that I'd wind up taking a class, but by the end of that first evening, I knew I wanted to learn more about such a wonderful thing. So I took the first level class, never thinking to go beyond that. (I've got two careers going now. I'm not about to add Reiki Practitioner to my list of jobs!)

The Many Faces of Journaling

But I have the strongest feeling that it's right for me to take the classes, and I'm now signed up for the next level training. I have no idea why I'm supposed to be doing this, but if I never use it to help others, if the only (!) benefit is this wonderfully peaceful, joyful feeling inside my own heart, it's totally worthwhile!!!!! I seem to see other people in a much less judgmental light, and to generally feel good and happy. How can that not be reason enough? Still I wonder if there's something else I'm supposed to do with it some time or other. Time will tell!!

(~ a Reiki Master)

Life Philosophies

From time to time we encounter chunks of wisdom that help us build our own unique life philosophy. We may run across them in reading, traveling, listening, or simply in the general process of living. As you find your own individual perceptions taking shape, record them. Such is the essence of the human experience.

These bits of personal religious philosophy come from the journals of Ralph Waldo Emerson:

March 1838 (age 35)

In the wood, God was manifest, as he was not in the sermon. In the cathedralled larches the ground-pine crept him, the thrush sung him, the robin complained him, the cat-bird mewed him, the anemone vibrated him, the wild apple bloomed him...the faint sharp-horned moon sailed steadily west through fleets of little clouds...

(~ Ralph Waldo Emerson)

March 1846 (age 42)

God builds his temple in the heart on the ruins of churches and religions.

(~ Ralph Waldo Emerson)

The Many Faces of Journaling

Over the course of a lifetime, we stretch and grow in so many glorious ways! Keeping a personal record of the dreams, goals, forward movement—even the disappointments allow us to look within and see the fine inner self who has always been actively involved in one way or another.

Chapter 3

Therapeutic Journaling

Our emotions are the driving powers of our lives.
When we are aroused emotionally,
unless we do something great and good,
we are in danger of letting our emotions become perverted.

— Earl Riney

Life is just chock full of emotional ups and downs. Fortunately, most of them fall into the category of minor occurrences and require little more than a grin or a groan. Unfortunately, many of our responses either get stuffed or don't lend themselves to easy resolution even if we are able to identify them.

Enter journaling. Psychotherapists and counselors have long recommended journaling to their clients as a part of the healing process. There are many advantages to this adjunct approach to the counseling process.

First it gives clients a positive way to actively participate in their therapy. Going to a therapist once a week can leave us feeling stalled between appointments, and employing the same old ineffective coping mechanisms often gets us nowhere. Journaling provides a fresh, proactive tool for healing.

There are various ways to utilize journaling to achieve good emotional health. We'll cover a number of them here. Try each one when and for as long as it feels appropriate. If you're accustomed to working on a computer, you may find that you can keep up with your speed of thought better by keyboard than with a pen and paper. If you find that to be true for you, by all means use your computer.

Before you key in the first page, though, be sure you know (or find out) how to password-protect a file. You may not care today if anyone else reads your entries, but tomorrow may be a different story. Besides, people do occasionally misinterpret what we say and write!

Be sure to include unlined paper—a sketchpad or plain copy paper—and colored pencils, markers, crayons, or soft sketching pencils in your journaling arsenal. You can often release a lot of emotion through the use of color.

Valuing Your Journal as a Friend

"Morgan," a college student at the time this entry was written, already appreciated the therapeutic value of keeping a journal.

November 29, 1990 ~1:28 p.m.

Well, it's time to get serious about journaling. There's too much crap running around in my brain, and I need to trap some of that chaos on paper. I need an organized, systematic, regular journal in which I can find solace, relief, support, and a general sense of having a handle on what's spinning wildly within the confines of my mind. I need to be HONEST, relatively OBJECTIVE, and KIND to myself in all my journeys within. I need to treat myself TENDERLY as a fruit blossom (yes, Thoreau). I want to list my goals and hopes and dreams and see the great things that fly right past me because I'm so caught up in b.s. worries. My journal gives me a sense of security-permanence and a reassurance that I'm getting in touch with myself.

(~ Morgan)

November 30, 1990 ~ 3:15 p.m.

I feel somehow privileged to be capable of seeing within myself this way. There are so many other college students here who are increasingly miserable and miserabler who don't know why. They spend all of their time blaming circumstances and avoid what's going on inside—what leads them into these circumstances time and again, how they handle the circumstances, what they glean from the experience afterwards. But they all think it's cool that I keep a journal. They say they just wouldn't know what to write. Maybe they just don't want to know?   (~ Morgan)

Ventilate

There are times in this life when you just can't say what you really feel. At least not out loud. Yet we all know by now that stuffed or misdirected anger can wreak havoc. If we shy away from our negative feelings, they build up in our subconscious minds like so much sewage. We can handle a certain amount, but too much can blow the lid off our mental health. If we feel the rage but are unable to deal directly with the offender, we often lash out at family and/or colleagues, causing even greater damage.

Writer Virginia Woolf vented her anger in this journal entry:

May 26, 1921

My evening being ruined by Grav as usual—I mean by
non-Grav—I mean she said she was coming at 6 & its
6.30—I may as well wreak my temper, write out my
fidgets, in this book. Such is the constitution of my brain
that I can settle to nothing if I'm waiting. This doesn't want
settling to. Haven't I schooled my diary well? It takes what
it can get & is thankful.   (~ Virginia Woolf)

"Ventilate & Incinerate" journaling provides an ever-available
release. Perhaps you feel frustrated beyond words at your boss's
absolute inability to see all aspects of a specific job. He tells you
to "just" work up a contract and get it signed, as though it were a
half-hour project.

Many times in the past you've pointed out the requisite steps
involved, including research into general industry policy, wording, costs, time required for completion of the work, penalties for
failure to meet the deadline, and so forth. Your boss knows them
as well as you do, but he chooses not to remember. And he
completely stonewalls you when you ask to go over the specifics
with him.

Going in to confront him when your knickers are all knotted up
could result in the loss of your job. (He has a hair trigger.) So you
have a choice: you can either dump it all into your journal or rage
at your family and have a quiet coronary.

Liberation through Incineration

The "incinerate" part of the Ventilate & Incinerate approach
provides you with an effective ritual for letting go of the past and
moving on with your life. This entry tells of the soul-deep release

and rebirth experienced by one journaler who carefully and thoughtfully burned several years' worth of personal journals.

Incineration

8/4/00 Poof—be gone! Free at last, free at last! I've torched the books full of who I was. Books full of suffering, humiliation, and foolishness. A funeral pyre in my Weber Kettle has left nothing of my lamentations but a sooty, black mess which I've swept under the hedges.

I'm lighter.
My baggage no longer so taxing

I'm looser.
Like doffing pinching heels at the end of a long day

I'm fresher.
Having let the waters of time rinse away life's grit

I'm freer.
A hefty elephant seems to have stepped off of my chest

I regret this no more than spring regrets the winter thaw.

(~ Anonymous)

Dialogue

Most of us already employ therapeutic dialoguing without thinking of it as such. Have you ever found yourself carrying on eloquent conversations in your head? The kind where you're finally able to say what you really mean or feel, and are able to answer all the questions that you imagine the other person might come up with? Or do you ever release colossal pent-up anger by mentally "saying" all those things you can't bring yourself to say to the person's face?

Once we give ourselves permission to actually feel angry about a person or situation, we can release enormous amounts of emotional tension by journaling such unspoken conversations. I find computer journaling especially effective for this, because for me it's much faster and closer to stream-of-consciousness than handwriting is.

In this example the journaler knew beyond a shred of doubt that her boss was an incompetent nincompoop, and also realized that saying these things to his face would cost her her job. So she let herself cut loose on her computer keyboard. (I've edited the salty language.)

Let Me Tell You!!!!

You did it again, you did it again, I swear to God I can't believe you walked all over my own hard work again today. And it was d____ good too — we both know that. And we both know, you total sack of ¬¬¬¬¬_____ that you couldn't have pulled that report together if you'd had all century to do it. You wouldn't have had the faintest idea where to start. You would have been too d¬¬¬¬____ dumb to ask for assistance or read a (gasp!) book on the subject so you wouldn't be so totally ignorant. IGNORANT IDIOT A_____ JERK!!! And I don't really give a ¬¬¬_____ whether you could do it or not cause I know you're my boss and I really DO love my job in spite of you you old ¬_____. But WHY WHY WHY couldn't you just for once give me the credit I deserve for doing a totally great job? Would it just kill you to tell the president that Sally did a fine job for us on this one??? Don't you know that would still reflect well on how you run your department? But NOOOOOOOOOO¬—you pretentious, phony, bag of wind, you pretender, you pathetic wannabee. You aren't capable of sharpening my pencils, but you sure are capable of taking all the credit THAT DOESN'T BELONG TO YOU!!!!!!

Many of us would have used seriously salty language just to let off steam, using words that we wouldn't ordinarily say out loud. Sometimes such impassioned language can be extremely effective in dialogue journaling. If you're doing this on a computer, try kicking the type size up to a 48- or 72-point size (normal is 10 or 12) and using bold lettering. It feels a lot like shouting at the top of your lungs. Please keep such entries in a very secure, private place. If discovered by the wrong person, they could come back to haunt you.

Cathartic

Therapeutic Journaling has long been a standard part of psycho-therapy, sometimes using words, other times employing the sketchpad and pencil. Its value in uncovering long-hidden emotions and attitudes and in venting pent-up anger and pain is well established. Anyone who's glommed onto a pen and paper or sat down at the keyboard at three o'clock in the morning to have a silent, vitriolic conversation with a problem person in his or her life, knows how much anger and grief can be unabashedly aired without the danger of anyone else reading our thoughts.

Mindy, then 16 years old, wrote this entry at a time of extreme personal pain:

Death

Tonight it became painfully apparent to me the magnitude of loss the world has sustained. My sweet friend Sarah was killed this afternoon. Shot in the face at point-blank range by her best friend. They were only playing, he thought the gun he was carrying wasn't loaded, he placed the barrel in front of her face and pulled the trigger. He was wrong; one bullet accidentally left in the chamber and a little girl is dead. I will never forget the feeling this day stamped upon me, just as I will never forget the wave of

nausea that nearly knocked me down when I learned of
this tragedy. I miss her. I feel for her parents, they are
devastated beyond rationality...[it is] a room full of
teenagers, my friends, just sitting and staring straight
ahead, clutching their sick stomachs and dabbing tears
from eyes that can't even cry anymore. That is death. That
is the full, unrelenting tragedy of it.

Everything now is so intense and overwhelmingly sad.
That's the funny thing about death. You never shed tears
for the one filling the grave, you cry for the one who
mourns their passing. I am aching for the mother who
screams violently that her baby will wake up any minute.
For the father who saw his little girl's lifeless body laying in
a hallway covered in blood. For the brother who just sits in
a corner continuously petting his dog because it is the only
thing he's sure of.

It strikes me with sadness and a keen sense of irony that
the little boy who took the life of his best friend should do it
on his 13th birthday. It was the day his life began and
ended all at once.   (~ Mindy Gramling-Bailey)

Such writing usually yields deep personal insights and can be a
valuable aid in healing.

Transitions

We can gain great perspective and comfort by journaling about our
rocky life transitions as we experience them. It allows us to
rummage around in our discomfort and search for the worst sore
spots. That, in turn, gives us specifics to work on, which is many
times more encouraging than floundering around in nameless fears
and fury.

It also helps us track our progress. This slightly abbreviated excerpt is from the journal of a woman who had just left her 26-year marriage and moved out of her home two weeks before. As she recorded the day's activities, she realized that, in an effort to help her soon-to-be-ex deal with the separation, she was spending far too much time either with him or talking to him on the phone.

October 24, day 14

While they were putting the new battery in my car, I walked up to Steak n Shake where [my soon-to-be-ex] met me…we talked about everyday things – nothing stressful, although anytime we talk or sit down together it's stressful for me because I'm never quite sure if some really tough stuff may come up, or if he'll just completely lose it & fly into an uncontrollable rage…he insisted on walking back to Dobbs with me. (He always thinks they're going to rip me off.) They charged me the minimum they and I had discussed and didn't recommend any further work – so there!

We went back to the house together for a little while so I could finish packing the piles of books from my bedside shelves to take back to my place…[that evening] watched the second half of the Jacquelyn Smith movie, and about 10:30 [husband] called me…to talk about us going to the first joint counseling session tomorrow.　　(~ Anonymous)

As she sat writing the above in her journal, she realized that, in an effort to be kind, she was sending out the wrong message, and that he might misinterpret her helpfulness as meaning she wished they were back together again. At that point she made up her mind to limit the amount of "buddy" contact they had. The act of journaling had provided invaluable perspective, which can be hard to come by during emotional upheaval.

The Many Faces of Journaling

Journaling can also allow us to ruminate on our sudden insights and to acknowledge the reasons behind current and prior behaveiors. In the following entry, the author of the above passage began to understand some of her earlier motives and actions.

October 29…day 19

Took a nap, and went for a 1/2 hour walk. Wish I had more energy – I really want to get back to regular exercise! When I was still at home, walking provided a significant escape, so I'd just keep walking for longer and longer periods until I was up to an hour because I didn't want to go back home again. Every time I went for a walk back then it was to get away from [my husband]. Now I have nothing to run away from.   (~ Anonymous)

Many of our major transitions are beginnings, not endings. Here a young bride-to-be ruminates on her coming nuptials:

On Getting Married

So here it is, and full of tears and indecision this little girl is. I cried all the way from Columbia to Sturgeon for my last night's rest in the Bailey [husband-to-be's family] house as a Gramling [her maiden name]. Hours, minutes, seconds are all that lie between me and forever adulthood. Forever as a wife, friend, daughter-in-law, maybe even a mother someday. I am reeled by this.

I never thought I would be a wife. I guess I never really thought I would live long enough to make much out of my life, never mind a home and family. Pessimism has its ugly claws deep in me. I called it "realistic expectations" and cowered under a line of gloomy poetry that made it okay to be sad and cynical all the time.

I think this might be a strange place to spend the night before one's wedding, sitting in the dimly lit living room of your fiancee's parents' house and lamenting the loss of a young girl, very, very puppy young girl in shoes that are way too large for her feet…I am a woman now, a full-fledged, card-carrying member of the ostensibly sensible clique of adults this world houses. Jody [fiancee] sleeps peacefully down the hall, the world turns ungreased on its axis and I sit in an uncomfortable chair with butterflies in my stomach.   (~Mindy Gramling-Bailey)

Moving certainly qualifies as a major life change, and like other such overwhelming adventures, the details, agonies, and pernicious upheaval of the move blur as time goes on. This entry by author and veteran journaler Mary Stuart (co-author of *The Divorce Recovery Journal*) illustrates the confusion and upheaval she experienced during her cross-country move from St. Louis to Phoenix.

June 24, 1999

I've had better days. I look forward to having them again, hopefully sooner rather than later. Living with friends who are also trying to pack up and move has added to my already considerable confusion, resulting in my not being able to find anything. This stems from trying to stay out of their way. I went to work today looking like a bag lady who lives in a car…damned if I could find my jeans or anything that matched. Then there was the frantic search for my Dayrunner, which contains my entire life. Found the Dayrunner; still don't know where the jeans are although I suspect they're in a box on the way to my final destination.

It's been a long time since I've done a cross-country move, and I understand why. Like childbirth, if you remember the pain you'd never do it again. But I'm moving toward a new start and moving away from painful experiences, and I feel in my bones it's the right thing to do.   (~ Mary Stuart)

Stream-of-Consciousness (SOC)

For stream-of-consciousness (SOC) writing there are no rules, no pauses for thought, no lifting the pen off the paper, and no expected outcome—a technique that can provide the most amazing insights into your own mind! Be sure to date these entries, for it's often useful to see what events in your life coincided with your SOC entries.

The following excerpt certainly represents loose-jointed writing, but undoubtedly reflected a general restlessness or ennui in the author's life.

Mental Ramblings

Someday it is going to be summer again but not for 100 years. Why do men send women flowers instead of bananas or shoelaces? My black dishes are getting on my nerves. They are so fat and heavy. I'm tired to the point of death from all these jagged and worrisome things. All of my skirts are getting too loose and ill-fitting. Oh, and I have forgotten the last name of the mayor of Vigo in the play *Les Miserables*. My mind is becoming old, dull, listless and lusterless. I believe it is time to read *The Little Prince* once again and maybe then Franny and Zooey. My spirit is becoming weak from lack of whimsy and overabundance of practicality.   (~ Mindy Gramling-Bailey)

SOC journaling is a useful tool for better understanding our fears, flaws, and foot dragging. Suppose you feel unaccountably sad or stubborn or unwilling to do something that you know would be good for you. Simply realizing that your gut response doesn't fit the situation is a good start. Then you might sit down quietly with a pen and notebook, and begin writing something like this.

Why...

My therapist has told me more than once that I need to get some kind of regular exercise — walking, swimming, whatever — and take specific time out each week for some kind of play (besides sex!), and no doubt she's absolutely right. But I don't do any of it. You'd think I'd try to fit SOME of it in cause I know she's right — I'm sure those things would help me feel less depressed (and I DON'T want to put any chemicals in my body to fight the bad feelings) — let's see, I don't <u>want</u> to feel depressed I don't think, or do I?

Maybe I want the people around me and my family to see by looking at me that I'm feeling crappy and then will pay attention to me and will reach out to hug me and feel sorry for me and maybe feel sorry for something mean they might have done to me and will try to make me feel better. And that would feel SO GOOD!!!! I'm so totally starved for somebody anybody to hold me and care about how I feel. But if I look like I'm not depressed anymore they'll all think — oh, well she's just fine again, she doesn't need us to do whatever anymore, she's fine on her own — and I don't really want them to walk away again. I want to be hugged and taken care of...   (~ Anonymous)

You can spin off from one insight to another, sometimes learning more in a half-hour of stream-of-consciousness journaling than you have in months of conscious pondering. If you're in counseling, share these entries with your therapist. You may both learn from them.

The Many Faces of Journaling

Therapists often suggest excellent coping devices to their clients. If yours does, make note of them in your journal so you can revisit them from time to time.

This therapy story, originally related in *And Now We Dance: Journaling for the Woman Within* (Linda Senn [2001] p. 145), is one of the dearest lessons I learned from my own therapist, Dr. Pamela Nickels:

Natural Instincts

Pam told me to close my eyes and picture a wild creature. I did and saw a gentle doe grazing in a meadow. "Do you trust her instincts to keep her from danger?" Pam asked. "Yes," I said. "Try to see that yours are just as reliable and protective as hers," Pam said. And that's when I slowly started to trust my own instincts again.

Relationships

Of all the complex aspects of our personal lives, our relationships with others can be the most psychologically volatile, rewarding, taxing, exasperating, and fun. What a challenge! Interactions with our spouses, children, bosses, in-laws, siblings, parents, neighbors, lovers, and potential lovers all call for special wisdom and insights. Nowhere does the expression "change is the only constant" apply any better.

Each change in an existing relationship can leave us feeling temporarily off-balance, like the bubble in a level that must rediscover its center. Such shifts range from slight adjustments to ferocious emotional upheavals.

Journaling as a relationship develops and grows can often help you deal with later misunderstandings. Entries about fresh, potentially significant friendships will enable you to see your new friend more clearly than the rose-colored glasses of romance will allow later on as the relationship grows into something more. A later rereading of your first impressions also enables you to check your initial impressions for reliability.

An effective ground-zero entry about first impressions is a great place to start. I gathered these impressions of a new friend on our first get-acquainted coffee date.

First Date/First Impressions

Warm smile—looks a little unfamiliar like he's not used to using it very much—we discovered several people from church and from the counseling community whom we both know—I like the way he talks about his children and how important his time with them is to him. ("It's absolutely the high point of my week—it's what I look forward to the most.") —high academic and professional achievement but he doesn't seem to flaunt it—he made no offer to pay for my coffee which gave me mixed emotions.

I guess I still like for the guy to offer to treat me even if I know we'll be going Dutch. Taking a walk after coffee was comfortable, like we were both a little relieved to be moving around more or less freely. I didn't pick up any warm/affectionate signals, but maybe he's just reserved at first. We'll see.

Experiment for one year with making such entries about new friends of both genders, new neighbors, pastors, and others, and you'll have a solid basis for testing your initial, intuitive impressions of the key people in your life.

Therapeutic journals can be valuable tools for emotional growth and healing. They give us the chance to safely shake our fists toward heaven, shriek and yell and say awful things about ourselves and others in a safe way, and trace our progress in life transitions. Try it. You'll be amazed at how much emotional steam you can vent through the pen or keyboard!

Chapter 4

Upbeat Journaling

Good humor is a tonic for mind and body.
It is the best antidote for anxiety and depressions.
It lightens human burdens.
It is the direct route to serenity and contentment.

— Grenville Kleiser

❧

Celebrating life's positive moments, whether they be humor or personal accomplishments, pays interesting dividends. The more we focus on and open ourselves to the upbeat moments in life, the more frequently we encounter them.

The healing qualities of positive thinking are well known to the medical and mental health communities: oncologists encourage cancer patients to attend laughter clinics, and therapists trust laughter as one measure of good mental health. And Dr. Martin Seligman's Positive Psychology course at University of Pennsylvania is one of the most popular on campus.

Smilers

This is a simple one. The Smiler Journal lets you enjoy happy, whimsical moments over and over again. Watch for humor in your everyday comings and goings. Set an arbitrary weekly entry quota of 5 or 10 or 15 fresh items. As you become more adept in your quest, you'll begin to pick up on more and more amusing snippets. Unless you're blessed with an extraordinary memory, you'll need to buy a small spiral-bound notebook—the kind you can tuck in your pocket or purse—and keep it with you so you can jot things down as they happen. After a few weeks, you'll find you can get a real boost from a quick read-through of your entries—sort of re-smile reading.

Children, in all their innocence and candor, provide us with a never-ending supply of surprising, smiling moments. Here's one about my grandchild:

A Sharing Kind of Child

(Dec. 24th) Tonight after our wonderful family dinner, we were all sitting around the living room, on chairs and on the floor. Kev was getting a feel for our new camcorder, while I held my darling grandbaby Caitlin (who turned 6 months old today) in my lap. Caitlin has adopted a fingers-in-her-mouth position in which she inserts her middle and ring fingers in her mouth with the index and pinkie fingers outside the mouth – the same general way my dad held his fingers in his mouth to whistle.

Well, bless her heart, she thought that was so fine that she decided to share with her Nonni, and with her right hand in her own mouth, she stuck her left hand in mine, sort of draped over my lower teeth to suck on or not as I chose. While the rest of us laughed uproariously, dear little Caitlin continued to gaze serenely around the room. I guess she just thought I was in need of a little mouth comfort!

The Many Faces of Journaling

The very young are a continuing source of delight for their elders, especially those of the grandparently persuasion. As little Caitlin approached her first birthday, she developed a giggling passion for playing peek-a-boo.

Peek-a-Boo

(June 21st) Tonight I was re-introduced to peek-a-boo (or peep-eye, as we used to call it) through the performance of my darling Caitlin, who is both a dainty and determined wisp of a girl child! (Now that she's walking, she refuses to crawl at all. What's she in such a hurry for?)

I'd forgotten how delirious little ones get when they first learn how to play peek-a-boo, but she sure did remind me tonight. First, she's simplified the whole process of hiding by just bending over. Obviously she figures if she can't see me, then she's hiding! Hey, it works for me.

Second, she has a little board book entitled Peek-a-Boo in her toy basket. She loves to have it read to her, and makes her request by whapping you in the nose with it. Well, I have to admit she got my attention. (And I was really glad it wasn't one of her hard cardboard books!)

Overheard

Eavesdropping can yield great smilers. Some are more fun out of context.

"Becoming wise shouldn't cause so many wrinkles.

Keep your "smiler's ear" open during sermons and church services. Today's clergy has to first capture our attention, then drive the point home. Humor does both. At an open forum discussion, one church member made his point by loosely quoting author-comedian George Carlin (*Brain Droppings*, Hyperion 1997):

> "Did you ever think, maybe the glass is neither half full nor half empty? Maybe it's just twice as big as it needs to be?"

Once you start recording these wise sayings, you'll discover lots of wonderfully uplifting snippets that you'll instantly want to incorporate into your philosophy of life.

My daughter, Heather, passed this one along to me. It holds a permanent place of honor on my computer desk.

Be Yourself

You should never have to
explain yourself.
Your friends don't expect it,
and your enemies won't believe you anyway.

Quotations

Quotation enthusiasts are bound to have a few bon mots and pithy sayings that set their heads to nodding each time they're reread. My co-author, Mary Stuart, and I included a number of our favorites in our book *The Divorce Recovery Journal*, including these:

> Courage is resistance to fear, mastery of fear –
> not absence of fear.   (~ Mark Twain)

> When you know and respect your own Inner Nature, you
> know where you belong.
>   (~ Benjamin Hoff in *The Tao of Pooh* 1983)

The Many Faces of Journaling

The heroic life is living the individual adventure.

(~ Joseph Campbell)

(and one of my all-time favorites)

Someday we'll look back on this moment and plow into a
parked car.   (~ Evan Davis)

My book *And Now We Dance: Journaling for the Woman Within*
also includes some spectacularly wise quotations:

Wisdom comes not from experience but from meditating
on experience and assimilating it.   (~ Joy Elmer Morgan)

The future belongs to those who believe in the beauty
of their dreams.   (~ Eleanor Roosevelt)

In between right and wrong is a soft, messy, laughing
place where it doesn't matter.   (~ SARK)

And a couple from my own book *And Now We Dance*:

We've become so focused on doing and accomplishment
that we've nearly lost the art of simply being.

Others don't think about us nearly as much as we suppose
they do. They're too busy wondering what we think about
them.

Thumbs Up

I wish I could explain why some of us feel uncomfortable
acknowledging our accomplishments, while others have no trouble

claiming credit for their achievements (and ours as well!). But a great many people experience a certain reticence when it comes to giving themselves a thumbs-up.

If you fit the latter description, you may be able to initiate a change in attitude through positive journaling. It can still be surprisingly difficult to even write, "Hey, I did an exceptionally creative, effective job on that!" Never mind. Just keep at it.

The more reluctant you are to make these entries, the more you may benefit from scheduled journaling. Create a set quota for yourself—perhaps three Way to go! entries a week with the understanding that they don't have to be earth-shaking accomplishments. Our lives are made up of many small successes for which we need to take credit. Setting a quota will force you to pat yourself on the back for both the minor and the grand.

A few years ago our minister, Reverend Janet Pillman, gave a beautiful sermon about how we can all be saints (with a lower case "s") by making a conscious effort to be kind in small ways. So remember to jot down your smaller kindnesses as well as your major achievements.

Thoughtfulness

Mar. 14th...I'm really getting the hang of using e-mail to make others feel good. I sent free e-greeting cards to Cheryl (Caribbean Cruise) and Mary (a week in London and environs) just before each of them left for their trips. I e-mailed the "thank you" that was in my heart to my healing touch friend. And I wrote to another congratulating him on his promotion. How good it feels to make others feel good about themselves!

Remember to give yourself points and journal the occasion when you go out of your way to honestly compliment somebody.

The Many Faces of Journaling

Cool Display!

Well, I managed to startle the ever-so-controlled manager of the men's department at Famous-Barr [department store] today. As I walked through the department waiting for D___ to find a jacket he liked well enough to try on, I was struck by the tabletop and counter displays – they were absolute works of art in color combinations, arrangement, texture, and so forth. You really wanted to stop and look. And I thought, well, shoot, somebody here must have done that. So I snagged this very proper manager, and told him how much I appreciated the artistry and taste of the displays in his area. His somber face broke open into the sweetest, warmest smile. Then he told me they were his doing. It's pretty cool when you can make somebody happy just by saying the truth out loud!

Obviously some of our entries will come from atta-girls and atta-boys at work. They count as much as the social entries.

Operation Snowball

Nov. 18, 1999…My boss is all excited about my marketing proposal -- Operation Snowball (as in snowball effect)! She wants me to go ahead and present a game plan for the next 6 months. She gave me certain guidelines about what kind of target cities she wants to hit, and told me to find half a dozen that fit her profile. She actually winked at me and said if the results (sales) increase as much as she thinks they will from my plan, there could be a nice bonus in it for me!!! Way to go me!

Web Site

August. 14th…I did it—I did it—I did it! I managed to figure out the horrible glitch in my newly created web page and I FIXED IT. It took nearly 2 days, and I got so discouraged the first day, I almost cried. (Some business woman, right?) If the HTML had refused to fall into place where Netscape seemed to want it, I knew I could go to Judy for emergency web treatment. But I wanted to be able to do it myself. AND I DID. Part of it was my fault, part of it was just the screwy, territorial servers. But I'm sure proud of me for being able to solve the messy problem!!!

Sometimes it's the boss who hears the feel-good comment.

Great New Job

My goodness…here I've been afraid of dumping too much new information on [my new employee] all at once, when I realized she actually/really enjoys this work. Today she told me that she's been going around telling her friends about this "totally cool new job" she has. That's so terrific! She likes the work and likes working here!

Whimsical Insights

From time to time our minds come up with unexpected insights and clever interpretations of life. A play on words may pop up into our consciousness and make us chuckle, or we may suddenly see a difficult situation in a new and amusing light. Capture the attendant words and phrases, and include them in your journal. Such entries are often rich in parodies and analogies, as is the following example:

Just Thinking

It was odd tonight, the air and all. A little misadventured I guess you could say. Life is on an even keel, at least I feel a little numb and nothing is pinching. I used to let things hurt me so deeply, I guess I still do at times. Everyone has

those Ivory Soap kind of days, you know when everything
imprints itself into you like a key into a bar of soap...
(~ Mindy Gramling-Bailey)

Heather was in a fun-silly mood when she wrote this.

Whimsy

Monk-ian around,
Angular and whole tone
Quirky dissonance
Thelonius.

(~ heather)

Or this journal entry that I wrote as a forty-something-year-old, as
I watched my children play in the back yard and remembered my
own tomboy days in the sun.

That Little Imp

When I think to myself
Of the imp in me,
I think of that imp
As a he not a she.

I think of it not
At a party with tea,
But of climbing a maple
And skinning a knee.

He's not at all proper
But blithe and carefree,
And that's just the way
That I want us to be.

The Many Faces of Journaling

Most of us have no trouble at all remembering times when we fell victim to the dreaded foot-in-mouth disease. You know—like the time you gave out with a side-splitting hee-haw-style laugh in the quiet theater, then realized you'd misunderstood the dialogue, which was actually quite tragic. Those stories make wonderful human-nature smilers, even if you were the one making the blunder. And it's so healthy to be able to gently laugh at our own goofs!

Keep a small notebook with you when you're out and about so you can capture those smiler moments when they come long. You'll treasure the good humor of the entries for decades to come.

Chapter 5

Creativity Journaling

*Imagination
is the secret reservoir
of the riches
of the human race.*

— Maude L. Frandsen

To paraphrase Webster, creativity involves producing something new and original through one's imaginative skills. We employ and nurture our creativity in an infinite number of ways from child-rearing to bridge-building, and journaling our progress through such original work can be both validating and enlightening.

This chapter focuses specifically on word play. What falls into this category? Altering definitions or inventing new ones; making up word games and quizzes; writing poems, songs, pithy or amusing essays on serious or absurd topics; and generally exploring a variety of mind-stretching ideas.

Some challenges will be pure fun. Others will tap into your inner self in fresh ways. Their purposes are pleasure and fulfillment through creative journal writing.

Poetry

Poems wear many different faces, from traditional metered rhyming verses to free style to the formal structures of Haiku. All are grist for the journaling mill. Some types may seem to lend themselves to a particular theme more than others. This is *your* project. Wax lyrical. Wax silly. Wax philosophical. Do all three. Edit your creative poems later to improve them or just leave them alone. This is playtime!

Inventing nonsense verses can lift the spirit, while helping you hone your style. Practice using colorful, specific words rather than bland generalities.

Mmm-m-m

Apricots and daffodils,
Pinot noir and thyme.
Everyone has fav'rites.
Those are some of mine.

Soul Food

Curses upon all of them,
The slender and the svelte.
A Hershey bar does my heart good
Until it hits my belt.

Free verse poems don't rhyme or have any set meter, but the best ones have rhythm and flow that come from the conscious use of words that "feel good in your mouth." They may express deeply felt emotions, keen life perceptions, worries, or humor.

My son Kevin, creator of the following piece, wrote, "My apologies to the book of Genesis, but I always figured the creation of the universe was a bit more chaotic."

Creation Story

"God woke up on Day One
And noticed there seemed to be rain clouds in the sky
He thought, "Ah, great! Another rainy day!
I guess I'll build a world while I let things dry."

But God was kinda clumsy on Day Two
He always seemed to find his bedpost with his shin
He thought about the photon, waves, and pain
So he invented light and heroine

He had a dream that second night
So when Day Three came he knew what to do
He dreamed about a frog that lived in his pocket
So he invented the kangaroo

God invented NyQuil on Day Six
He tried it out with the angels in Heaven
And with all that NyQuil running through their heads
They figured they'd better just rest come Day Seven"

(~ Kevin T. Tisdel)

For a time, he was on a real birth/creation kick. Writing about things that seem to spring from nothing is sort of meta-writing, since creativity and writing often are 'seedless.' Such is the following piece:

Birth Time

Safe and sound, warm and cozy
No home like the inside

No fears
Can't be afraid of a snake
When I don't know what a snake is
I float like a ghost
Swim like a fish
I'd wish upon a star
If I could see one
Dreams of colors
Dreams of voices

And then a feeling of anticipation
Clocks were ticking
Fingers were tapping
Today isn't going to be like any other day
One moment: darkness
And now this.

The first introduction is made
"Child, this is light. Use it well."
"Light, this is your gift for shining–a child of mine."
And then a peering head
My first breath
Independence of sorts
And that voice–the only familiar experience
Since entering this existence
That is remotely familiar
Cling to the voice
Follow the voice
Learn the voice
It means life
It means dependence
(Not as free as I once thought)
What a crazy thing it is to be alive
What a crazy thing it is to live–to feel the sun
Still no thoughts, because there are no words to code
    thoughts in,

But shapes, and colors and sounds are enough
Thoughts would only confuse things
What I see is purity of light and form, unobstructed by the
limitations
Of the vocabulary of humanity
No bias
No pre-conceived notions about what something is for or
who a person is
    I see things as God himself sees them
    I am a newborn
    I am your God
    I will not judge, only be judged with apathy
    Contaminate me as you will in your own time
    Make me one of the impure
    I will spend the rest of my life
    Fighting to feel as alive as I feel
    This very moment.   (~ Kevin T. Tisdel)

Free verse poetry lends itself to both beauty of form and elegance of perception. The cadence and flow of the syllables creates its own mood, and the words themselves can be used both to build and to catch the reader by surprise, as this poem shows:

Loneliness

Loneliness falls
    not with butterfly wings
    but with a smack
    of eagle's talons –
gripping,
suffocating,
with pain
that stills the soul.

It is a loathsome thing,
   this invisible suppression
   which leaves the heart
      shaken and afraid,
       despairing of its duration;
  for it's one thing
  to be lonely alone,
  but agony to be lonely
      with you.
          (~ Beverly J. Letchworth)

Such poetical ruminations may be the creation of a very young mind as well as of the more experienced, mature journaler. Mindy was eighteen when she wrote this:

Mindy's Poem

A climax of all unordinary things the cliquish night was—
It bled to death the last purple drops of day.
And if anyone has ever seen a sun set like it wasn't
Setting at all...
I thought it a good time to think—
So I let my guard down and put my imagination on the plank.

It wondered slyly for a moment and–in time–
Surrendered itself to reading what poets do not write.
And as I can only begin to think it seemed a fine thing to me.

The air was cold (it could be warm if I wanted it to)
The night was full of things imaginations love—
Goblins, fireflies and the musical styles of Lute's flute.
All the air was pierced and sweet-smelling from
The Lilacs blooming out of the snow
And deep in the background
was something I knew to be wisdom—

The Many Faces of Journaling

Only I couldn't see it clearly from where I stood.
It was riding a dragon.
(~ Mindy Gramling-Bailey)

Because Haiku, Tanka, and Cinquain verse forms are based on counted syllables, they often appeal more to linear thinkers, especially the math-oriented folks, than free verse style. Such word art employs both the right (creative) and left (linear) halves of the brain.

Haiku, the lovely Japanese verse form, has three lines with syllable counts of 5-7-5. Traditional haiku usually has a nature theme, as the following verse does:

Snow

Snowflakes drifting down,
Pure and holy on my tongue —
Winter's sacrament.

A **tanka** is an expanded haiku containing five lines with syllable counts of 5-7-5-7-7. Often one person writes the first three lines, and another adds the last two. Here is an example:

Night

The banked fires of day
Gently lead the soul to rest —
Sunset's amber glow,
Thence the sooty, soft nightfall
Preceding the pearl of dawn.

Cinquains have five lines with syllable counts of 2-4-6-8-2. It's fun to build verse upon verse in the cinquain style. There's no real reason not to be playful with haiku, but for some reason, the cinquain form seems to lend itself more to whimsy.

Not Cool

Mister,
What can I say?
I know you think you're cool
Because your Mama told you so.
She's wrong.

Essays and Prose

Journal writing can be a marvelous vehicle for building creativity if you explore the ordinary in a thoroughly extraordinary way. Push past your ingrained, "normal" ideas, and try writing journal entries based on these ideas:

▶▶ Write a fictional essay on:

1. why butter melts.
2. the benefits of being able to walk up walls.
3. what person, object, book, and musical instrument you'd want with you on a desert island if you were going to be there a week? a month? a year?

▶▶ Write a glowing letter of recommendation about some person in your office, family, or neighborhood who really grates on your nerves! (You may have to make it semi-fictional!)

▶▶ Write a news article announcing that your pet (cat, dog, hamster, turtle, rock, Teddy bear, etc.) has just confessed to being an ambassador from another planet, and tell how you know that to be a fact. (Include a mock interview with fascinating quotes.)

▸▸ Write a story or paragraph about one of the following words (using any definition that tickles your fancy):

Aha!	face	hit
bay	first	mass
bean	glaze	miss
bliss	halt	master
box	harp	mole
corner	healing	radical
dot	hero	swirl
Earth	hiss	up

You can vary your word play with the above list by experimenting with the following:

1. Use one word from each list in your journal entry.
2. Include all the words from one list.
3. Include as many words from the total list as you can.
4. Now try the above (#3) using as few additional words as possible.
5. Create your own list(s) of 20-25 words, including several with multiple meanings.

▸▸ **Are you a natural storyteller?** Create a new-age fable with yourself as the hero by using a combination of fact, fantasy, and anything else that's handy. Now write one about each of your friends and give them their own fables as presents!

▸▸ **Instant observations.** Sit in any room of your home, in a park, at work, or in the middle of a football field. Close your eyes for a few seconds, and when you open them, write about the first object or person you see.

Lyrics

Just as some people gravitate toward prose or Haiku, the musically inclined among us pour out their emotions and creativity into writing song lyrics. These usually tell a story, reflect a personal dilemma or philosophy, or offer a parody on life in general.

Matt Carlock, drummer/singer/songwriter for the band Ghost Junction, wrote this song. It's a favorite of many of his fans and appears on the band's first CD, Ghost Junction (2000):

Selfish Tune

I like it dark in here
please turn off the light
no, not even a candle
it would be too bright
inside...this
selfish tune of
mine

please would you go away
so I can miss you some more
I hate your kind remarks
but leave a note on the door
outside...this
selfish tune of
mine

wild winds are
blowing thru the yard
I search for sadness in the trees
think back to yesterday
I've always been this way
do you feel sorry for me?
I like to taste the tears
and count them one by one

I write the total down
mail it to everyone
outside...this
selfish tune of
mine

I took your picture down
because you stare at me
and then I cut out your eyes
so full of sympathy—
those eyes, won't
light up this tomb of
mine

I hear you call to me
"Let's go away for a while"
I'm soaking in myself
I'm sitting Indian style
inside...this
selfish tune of
mine

wild winds are
blowing thru the yard
I search for sadness in the trees
think back to yesterday
I've always been this way
do you feel sorry for me?

(~ Matt Carlock)

Word Play

All kinds of playful forms, including puzzles, games, and quizzes, can be creativity builders. Have you ever tackled the code puzzles where you have to figure out the title, phrase, or quotation from a combination of letters and numbers?

Code Puzzles

1ibl 2ibs (answer: one if by land, two if by sea)

60miah (answer: 60 minutes in an hour)

101D (answer: *One-Hundred and One Dalmatians*)

W3KoOA (answer: *We Three Kinds of Orient Are*)

12miay (answer: 12 months in a year)

TfT (answer: song title *Tea for Two*)

7WotW (answer: Seven Wonders of the World)

3RC (answer: Three-Ring Circus)

50WtLYL (answer: song title *50 Ways to Leave Your Lover*)

They're fun to make up, and great to pass around as a challenge to your friends.

Beverly J. Letchworth, author of *Leaf Bird Days & Firefly Nights: Personal Renewal Through Nature Journaling* (2001), uses a playful technique to help her writing students think outside the box. She asks them to write about the smell of blue and the color of violin music. What a shock to our long-held points of reference! Try your hand at writing a paragraph or two about the following:

▶▶ Describe the smell of:
- aqua
  - a sunset
    - classic guitar music
      - concrete

▶▶ Describe the sound of:
- grapes
  - gray
    - a rose bud
      - snow falling

▸▸ Describe the color of :
- jingling
  - echoes
    - pain
      - tart

Creativity applies not only to word play, but also to painting, sculpting, carving, writing a software program, interior decorating, landscape architecture, growing bonsai trees, building a log cabin, and all other areas that challenge us to use innovative, original thought to create something new.

Journal your progress in any creative endeavor, making note of when you start and complete the project, and the problems, joys, and lessons learned. Keep a list of materials used, where you obtained them, the cost, and your evaluation. And of course, record the way you *feel* at each step along the way. Hopeful? Excited? Crestfallen? Irritated? Exhilarated? Any creative journey offers valuable opportunities for better understanding your own hopes and uncertainties.

Snippets

This kind of record might include brief word pictures of people or events, thought-provoking phrases from overheard conversations, and the seeds of ideas for a whole host of future writing projects.

Spiral notebooks have always appealed to me for this kind of project. They're inexpensive, so you can doodle and waste space without a trace of guilt, and they do have a "work in progress" feel to them.

This kind of journaling grows in direct proportion to the frequency of use. The more you jot down those fascinating ideas, the more often you'll remember to do so. Sometimes when you hear a song, a parody pops into your head. Don't let it get away. Write it down!

Such entries will range from two or three fertile words to full thoughts, like these:

Snippet Samples

- ▸ the wrinkled, old face of a little boy, his anguished
- ▸ eyes searching her face for love
- ▸ something gone—something gained
- ▸ sooty soft
- ▸ "Follow your bliss." (~ *Joseph Campbell*)
- ▸ not old, but a wise woman of the tribe
- ▸ little helium balloons bouncing around my heart
- ▸ a whole-grain kind of woman
- ▸ Scarab—an ancient symbol of protection, long endurance, stamina

Over the years you'll build a wealth of excitingly varied notes, some of which will lead to the writing of poetry or prose. And you may find that simply reading over them is a delicious pleasure in and of itself.

Chapter 6

Scrapbook Journaling

Remember as far as anyone knows, we're a nice normal family.

— *Homer Simpson*

However simple or elaborate the pages of a modern scrapbook may be, the photographs thereon show only the visual aspect of that instant. Without an accompanying written entry, the photos of Johnny's birthday party may seem to speak for themselves. But they don't show the smile in his heart as he anticipates getting that wiggly new Heinz 57 puppy in a few hours.

The photo also can't show the Sesame Street music, hot popcorn smell, or the other textures, flavors and moods of the event, nor of the weird weather or off-camera shenanigans. But words can.

Getting the Right Look for Your Journaling Entries

How and where to include your written entries varies according to the topic and general layout of the scrapbook. One school of thought says handwritten entries add a special personal touch. This works best if you have reasonably clear handwriting and if the entry isn't too long. It's also an effective technique for pithy quotations or a short poem.

You can add variety to these by using different kinds of pens – felt-tipped, calligraphy, ball point, or an old fashioned fountain pen, and select ink colors to compliment your page design.

With typed entries, you can fit more words into a smaller space, which lends itself to full-page and scene-setting journal entries.

You can choose the font to suit the mood of the page.

- The Curlz font is fun for party pages.
- One of the script fonts gives the flowing impression of a hand-written entry.
- And there are lots of playful artistic fonts like MATISSE, Alba Mabber, and Fiolex Girls .

If you have a color printer, you can add variety to your typed entries. But be careful that the colorful journaling entry doesn't become so elaborate that it competes with the scrapbook artistry.

Don't rush through the writing and installation of your entries. Instead, stick a bright Post-It note on the page to mark the Future Journaling Space. Then write the entry, set it aside for a day or two, read over it, and rewrite it one last time to refine it.

As for the paper on which you write or print the scrapbook journal entry, a visit to your local craft and scrapbooking stores, or even a large copy shop will reveal a tantalizing array of parchment, marbled, variously textured and plain paper in colors ranging from eye-popping Astro Brights to the gentlest pastels. The choices will delight and confuse you!

Before you write or after you print, the edges may be left clean or be carefully torn to create a ragged edge. Or you might enjoy experimenting with wavy, zigzag, or other design effects using special scissors or paper cutters.

The written journaling piece can be framed on the page with anything from popsicle sticks to small feathers to lace, rickrack, or other trim from craft stores, scrapbooking supply shops, or the fabric store. You can also use a medium to large template, cut a window in a page from an appropriate travel, children's, or décorating magazine or a special kid-created, painted or crayon-drawn picture.

The Kinds of Information to Include

Short entries can be placed beside the photo, or two or three might be interspersed among several photos on a single page. These generally elaborate on the people and scenes depicted in the photos.:

Young Taylor's mom wrote this scrapbook journal example telling him about the Monty and Pipsqueak stories his Grandma Rose used to tell him::

Monty and Pipsqueak

When you were about two-years-old, you loved for me or Grandma Rose to tell you stories. One day your Grandma Rose invented Monty and Pipsqueak. Monty was a mongoose your age and Pipsqueak was his younger sister. They lived with their mom and dad and on occasion, if the story was interesting enough, you would join them on their adventures. After a while, Grandma Rose ended up with some different characters and I inherited Monty and Pipsqueak. You didn't care what they did, as long as I was telling the story. They have been to a volcano, swimming, gymnastics practice, Costa Rica, Florida, Football practice, school, the movies, playing putt-putt, pretty much anything that we have done or that you find interesting, they have done. Anytime we are alone and you are bored, you always ask "can you tell me a story about Monty and Pipsqueak?" And if I am not too tired and I can let my mind wonder, we start a new adventure.   (~ Cathleen Castillo)

Was there unusual weather just before or after the photos were taken? That was the case at this birthday party:

Taylor's 7th Birthday Party

While the children pounded away at an especially sturdy piñata, the parents watched the sky and gathered around the dad with the weather alert gizmo. You see, those dark clouds had already produced one tornado, and it was headed for this part of Green County. And as you kids scrambled around gathering up the goodies from the piñata, the grown-ups cleaned up and made ready to leave at a mach 3! As we all hit the parking lot, the weather siren started, scaring the bejeebers out of a few children. But everyone got home safely, and the tornado stayed up in the clouds. It's a good thing you had swim time before the birthday cake and presents. After all it was a pool party!

Put your longer entries on the page opposite the photos, and include additional details about the event, the preparations, names of the participants, location, or a special memory of the day.

The Many Faces of Journaling

Caitlin's 8th Birthday Party ~ 70s Theme

Who: Caitlin Elizabeth Gooferberry
What: 8th Birthday Party
When: June 23rd, 2007
Where: Her house at 1234 Alphabet Way
Guests:

Grandma D &	Ken
Peepaw	Arthur & Gabe
Nonni	Jenny & Jerry
Zander	Becca & Ben
Uncle Kev &	Briana
Aunt Cathy	Mary
Taylor	Joann

We had cheese and pepperoni pizza, soda, and pink and white birthday cake with ice cream. It took so long for Caitlin to open all her wonderful presents, that there wasn't enough time left for any games. But there were lots of cool balloons, streamers, party plates, and giggles. And disco music playing the whole time!

Quotations

For variety, you can use shorter entries, such as a pithy quotation, a line or two from a song, or a nifty quote from the person in the photo.

This quotation works well on a page about the family fishing vacation:

> God does not charge time spent fishing against a man's
> allotted life span.   (– American Indian Proverb)

Do you have a photo of a tangle of happy children writhing around on the floor? How about this quotation:

> Having a family is like having a bowling alley installed in
> your brain.   (– Martin Mull)

Scrapbook entries are also a fine place to honor and preserve special family sayings and nicknames. Some families strongly favor playful terms of endearment like sugar button, honey pot, baby dumplin', champ, and sport.

Adding Pizzazz to your Entries

Details make your written entries come to life. Smells, textures, sounds, tastes and emotions bring smiles to the reader – sometimes even giggles. Notice Cathy's wording: *squishy, rainbow, snuggly nestled beneath one of your arms* – even *drooled on* paints a beautiful word picture.

Fruit Stripe

For Christmas when you were five-years-old, I found you a squishy stuffed striped puppy in one of the bins at TJ Maxx. As soon as I spotted him, I knew he was perfect for you! He looked like a little rainbow. When you got him, I would have to say he was one of your favorite Christmas gifts. When we were trying to come up with a name for him, Kevin came up with "Fruit Stripe" like the gum we chewed as kids because his pattern is very similar. You adopted it for him and he has been Fruit Stripe ever since! He sleeps with you every night and even when I go in to check on you, he is snuggly nestled beneath one of your arms or being drooled on under your face. You do not like going anywhere to spend the night without him. He has become one of your best friends.   (~ Cathleen Castillo)

Descriptions of sounds can add even more depth.

Talking Bear

You were so tickled with the silky-soft, shaggy teddy bear you got for your second Christmas. At the Build-a-Bear shop, I'd made a recording which they placed in the bear's left paw. When pressed, it said, in my sweetest grandmother's voice, "Merry Christmas, Zander. Nonni loves you." And you did love hearing that. Unfortunately, you stared rolling over on it at night, pressing the button to start the recording. That woke everybody up and made it sound like I'd walked into your house in the middle of the night! So your Mommy started giving you a different toy for sleepy time. (~ Nonni)

No crowding! In writing your entries, be careful not to cram too many words on a small piece of paper. Dense text looks boring and can be harder to read. Leave a comfortable amount of blank space on the paper. If you're typing, put some extra space between lines.

Your Journal Entry As a Centerpiece

Occasionally you may want to make the written words the center-piece of the page.

The following "centerpiece" entry preserves memories of a loving family ritual that young Taylor can cherish all his life:

Bedtime Traditions

Each night at our house, we embark on a new and exciting adventure when it is time for you to go off to sleep. Once you have your teeth brushed and your pajamas on, we proceed with our rituals. We have an order that we follow each and every night. It starts with your dad and I coming in to make sure your pajamas are on and you are ready for bed. Pop starts with his rituals, and when he is done, I follow with mine.

And back….

Since I always say my goodnights after Pop, I usually take the time he is in there with you to go to the bathroom. When I finish with that, I sneak into your room so that you don't see me (although you usually know when I come in) and hide under your loft until Pop says, "and back…". The general premise behind these stories is that I've been off on a long and distant journey to some faraway land that is usually taken right out of one of our pieces of children's literature or fantasy literature.

We have made up stories from Egypt, the rain forest, Olympus, Atlantis, Neverland, Narnia, etc. The point is that he tells a quick story of a place that I have been to and am now just returning from and all the adventures I had in that place before I came back to tuck you into bed. We are always telling stories in our house, whether it be with made-up characters, stuffed animals that talk, or imaginary volcanoes…you devour each and every one. This one is a favorite of yours because you like the recollection of the familiar stories.   (~ Cathleen Castillo)

A poem you wrote or one that's especially dear to the honoree adds an extra bit of interest. On my wall is a lovely shadowbox that was constructed much like a scrapbooking page. In the center is the following poem I wrote about my maternal grandmother, Mam. It's printed on parchment paper and edged in lace. Around it are a photo of her and my grandfather when they were courting, an old fashioned postcard, a lock of blonde hair and assorted other bits. This poem fills in some of the sensory details – the special smells, sounds, and textures – that the photo can't convey:

Mam

Whenever I smell
    Southern fried chicken or Muguet cologne,
    Purple wisteria's heavy perfume,
    Cinnamon apple pies, scented sachets,
        Musty dark basements or cloves in the ham,
I remember my grandmother, Mam.

Whenever I see
    Christmas tree angels or curtained French doors,
    Bright gingham aprons cross-stitched 'round the hem,
    Pansies and bird baths and wishbones to pull,
        Rocking chairs, solitaire, wrinkled dry skin,
I remember my grandmother, Mam.

Whenever I think of
    Her twinkling blue eyes or her lacy trimmed hankies,
    Her watching the finches or humming for joy,
    Or sprinkling fairy fuel into the fire,
        Her all-loving aura, my touchstone, my friend,
I still miss my grandmother, Mam.

Scrapbooks are a perfect example of a legacy to be enjoyed now and treasured in years to come. Add that extra depth to your memories with warm and loving written scrapbook journal entries.

The Many Faces of Journaling

Chapter 7

Journaling for the Next Generation

There are only two lasting bequests we can hope to give our children. One of these is roots, the other, wings.

— *Hodding Carter*

༈

There are many legacies you can leave for your family's next generation. You might bequeath them the family silver, the stocks and bonds, and your Hummel collection, but there's something else that's far more intimate and loving than all of those things combined: your loving memories.

Think about the things you want to share with the next generation: your joy and pride in them as they grow, your warm recollections of your own childhood, and reflections on your life and place in the Universe. You can offer your family no finer keepsake than a sharing of yourself.

The Many Faces of Journaling

Journals for Posterity

These can be warm, personal messages addressed directly to them using "you," such as "Janey, when I was 6, like you are now, my Dad built the most wonderful high swing in the big maple tree out back." Or you can phrase the entries as personal musings using "I," like "I remember back in 5th grade, when my teacher showed us how to test food for carbohydrate content using iodine."

Pregnancy engenders great feelings of joy, fear, anticipation, and love in expectant parents. We're going to have a sweet baby child, our next generation, to add joy and laughter to our lives! Can I be a good mommy? Is everything ready? I've never felt this depth of protective love before in my life!

One of the dearest things an expectant parent or grandparent can do during the wait is to write a journal to the little-one-to-be. These baby journal entries were written by a young mother during her first pregnancy:

Dear Baby...

11/8/98   Dear Baby,
It's ironic that the most significant, most influential times of our lives are those we forget as we get older. We are dependent on someone's perspective—and the memory of that perspective—to help us understand our roots and our springtime of life. Knowing where you come from helps you decide where you want to go, and where you don't want to go. It gives you a sense of direction. I hope this journal helps.

11/20/98   Dear Baby,
I had a dream about you last night. You were tiny, tiny, and I had put you in a safe place. Only when I realized I needed to find you, I couldn't remember where you were. You were still as small as my pinkie finger. By the time I

The Many Faces of Journaling

finally found you, you were full baby-sized. I can't see you, but I trust that you're nestled safe and sound inside of me digesting those yummy prenatal vitamins. Bon apetit!

12/6/98   Dear Baby,
I'm so worried about being a good enough mom, that I'm forgetting to ENJOY expecting you! "Worryin' don't butter the bread!" I just want to give you the family and home you deserve. I already love you so much…but I'll never be the "perfect mom." I'll work on "pretty OK" though.

12/13/98   Dear Baby,
Congratulations! Today you became a full-fledged fetus! You're no longer an embryo. You even look like a real baby according to my book. You're about the size of my thumb. By next week you'll be as big as a large lime. Your heart beat is music to my ears! The doctor let me tape record it, so I've listened to it again and again. "Look! Sons are an inheritance from Jehovah; the fruitage of the belly is a reward" (Ps. 127:3).

2/10/99   Dear Baby Girl,
Your ultrasound was hilarious! You were punching and squirming and hiccuping! I saw the four chambers of your heart and the two hemispheres of your brain. You look perfect and lovely. I carry your ultrasound pictures around with me in an envelope, despite the fact that everyone else seems to think that they look like alien x-rays!

6/21/99   Dear Thumper,
You've gotten so big! I've gained 46 pounds. You've got to feel crowded in there! Your knobby little knees poke out my front and right side. There's no more room for them inside! Your bassinet is all ready for you with fresh blankets and a snugly soft sleeper. Your coming-home dress is packed and ready to go at a moments notice. We

The Many Faces of Journaling

have so many warm memories ahead of us! [Little
Thumper was born on June 24th.]   (~ Anonymous)

Family Stories

Children love to hear about what life was like when their parents,
aunts, uncles, and grandparents were small, and there's no richer
topic for such stories than family holiday traditions. Remember to
include the smells, the sounds, and the feel of the occasion, as well
as the sights. That kind of detailed sensory description helps the
reader more completely immerse him- or herself in the story.

Santa Bags

Oh, my Precious Grandbaby, what fun the Christmas
stocking ritual was when your Mom was little! The red brick
fireplace in the family room was perfect for hanging
stockings and setting out Spritz cookies and milk.

Then about the time they reached junior high age, I
decided to start a brand new tradition based on those
stockings, and our Christmas Santa Bags were born!
Ours were a lush, deep green velour, about 10" x 18", with
bright red and white braided drawstrings at the top. (I
sewed them up at night after the kids went to bed!) Using
fabric paint and brushes, each of us adorned our own bag
with our name and holiday decorations like Christmas
trees and gingerbread men.

Each one shopped for all three of the others in the family,
looking for both typical and surprise stocking stuffers.
These always wound up being the most thoughtful,
personal gifts of all. (We also collected freebies all year
long to help us stretch our gift allowances.)

Just before bedtime on Christmas Eve, we would go in to the living room, one by one, to put our unwrapped gifts in the appropriate bags. (We were on our honor not to peek inside our own.) In the morning, I was as excited as a four-year-old, and would roust everybody out of bed about 8:00.

In the living room we gathered, bundled in our snugly winter robes, sipping steamy coffee and eating the buttery-rich Pannetone. And slowly we would dip our hands into the Santa bags, drawing out one lovely surprise after another.

Over the years our Santa bags have offered up samples of cologne and after shave, puzzle books, rubber bands, cosmetics, pens, Hershey bars, miniature basketballs, playing cards, combs, paperback books, microwave popcorn, giant colored paper clips, nail files, fish lures, kazoos, and even one heart-shaped pumice stone.

The most wonderful part of this ritual was that each person put so much loving energy into thinking about the others' interests and preferences. And we all looked forward to the childlike thrill of Christmas Santa bags long after Santa Claus moved on.

In earlier times, family stories were usually passed from one generation to the next around the campfire or dinner table. Today families may be scattered all over the world, leaving precious little time for traditional storytelling. So other ways must be found for upholding tradition and reinforcing family identity.

You can make tapes of these tales and mail them to the children, but it takes a surprising amount of self-discipline to sit down with the tape recorder and relate your stories to a small inanimate object! An alternate method, of course, is to write the stories down.

The Many Faces of Journaling

Work up a family tree to give the children a sense of "tribe" and their place in it. Then write a story (or several) about each person on the tree who played a part in your own life. Make them come alive through colorful, animated storytelling. Genealogy is most interesting to the reader when those names become real people.

Ralph Waldo Emerson wrote this description of his aunt:

Aunt Mary

Boston, October 19, 1832 (age 29) My aunt [Mary Moody Emerson] had an eye that went through and through you like a needle. 'She was endowed,' she said, 'with the fatal gift of penetration.' She disgusted everybody because she knew them too well.   (~ Ralph Waldo Emerson)

This describes one of my favorite uncles, my Dad's older brother:

Uncle Bill

Wm. Lincoln Senn was relatively short and wiry like his Dad [my grandfather], and had the family's curly hair. He had the most glorious laugh, which he used a lot—it sounded like a happy Billy goat. He loved telling shaggy-dog stories (the really, really long ones with the groaner endings). He was the one who took all the family movies.

I remember curling up on the couch at his and Aunt Alberta's in the company of the rest of the Senn family to watch the latest in 8mm holiday movies. It was always nighttime, and I would be so sleepy in the darkened room, but I loved to revisit Christmas and all the fun holidays. In his college days, he played banjo with his own band. (Maybe that's where Kev got his gift for music.) That would have been in the Roaring Twenties, and I'm told he had a very active social life, and wore a raccoon coat which was quite the fashion at that time.

You can spice up the content by mixing narrative stories with poetry, quotes, sketches, and photos. My maternal grandmother, Vivian Gaunt Creecy, used many of the colorful expressions of her Arkansas childhood in her later years. Some that instantly bring her loving smile back to me are:

Facts are stubborn things. [*Not my favorite, but inevitably true*]

I cut out the wishbone just for you, Baby! [*She always remembered my preference when she cut up a chicken.*]

Mama, are you starting another quilt? [*My great-grandmother, Mannie, sat in her rocker and quilted by the hour as she listened to the radio soap operas.*]

Make the family history rich with your own memories, as well as stories about grandma's (and great-great-grandmother's) life, and family, including excerpts from the young bride's cookbook or her own journal. Start the process with your own childhood to prime the memory pump.

Beverly J. Letchworth, author of *Leaf Bird Days & Firefly Nights* (2001), tells this story from her childhood:

One With the Sky
Playgrounds and parks have swing sets. Many homes have swing sets. Squat, store-bought sets that all look alike and swing the same. I'm glad they're available, because they're a universal delight for children the world over.

But for the ultimate in true swinging with a capital S, give me the simple, old-time tree swings with their long, deep glides.

My family was lucky. We had a huge pear tree in the backyard with a stout limb that arched perfectly from the trunk, some fifteen feet above the ground. Over that support, Dad looped a thick rope. A wood plank, sawed and sanded smooth, made the swing seat. It was nothing fancy, but it carried our spirits to the sky.

Sit, push off with tiptoes, lean back as you pump with your legs. Higher, higher, until your head brushed the leaves. Now you could relax as you swooped down and back up, your feet kicking branches at the end of the arc. And in that glorious, air-rushing sweep, you soared like the birds. Sometimes we spun around and around until the ropes couldn't be twisted any tighter. Then raise feet and the swing took off, spinning around, faster and faster, until the ropes unwound in a last lunge of motion. I suppose we were dizzy at the end, but I can't remember much discomfort.

I invented another swinging option. In the swing, I moved to the tree trunk, raised my foot as high as I could to push against the trunk. This propelled me out and around in a wide arc that brought me to the other side of the trunk, where I'd repeat the maneuver.

But sometimes I didn't swing at all; I just sat on the swing seat and gazed up into the tree canopy. There, under an umbrella of green, I mused and daydreamed and simply was.

High technology has its place, but so do the so-called simple things in life. Sometimes that's all you need to bring

The Many Faces of Journaling

comfort and contentment to you soul. Oh, that every child today could have a tree swing and know what it feels like to be one with the sky!   (~ Beverly J. Letchworth)

Every family has long-ago favorite tales. They may be about ancestors who were horse thieves, pioneers, explorers, artists, or they may be wonderful love stories. Use the voice of a storyteller with the children gathered at your knee.

Emily and Theodore

This is a true family love story. The Buder family consisted of a strong and capable mother and (I think) four sons, all of whom became highly respected lawyers in the community. Great-aunt Emily Senn was their family's seamstress. She was the youngest of the four Senn siblings. She and Theodore Buder, who was likewise the youngest of those four brothers, fell in love, and evidently defying some negative attitude on his family's part, married. (That would have been sometime around 1900 give or take.)

It is said that his family showed their disapproval of this socially unequal love match by giving the couple nothing more than a shadowbox containing a rather elaborately decorated porcelain plate. [To my child's eyes it was both magical and magnificent, but I knew nothing of the relative monetary value.] That was the entire wedding gift from them. I would love to have known this courageous young couple – I think I would have liked them very much – but they both died young in the great influenza pandemic of the early 1900s.

Mutual Journaling with the Next Generation

An exciting, ongoing way to share both your memories and your daily life with a child is to keep a *two-generation journal* wherein both the older and the younger write their own entries in the same book, perhaps on facing pages.

Theoretically, you could simply pass the journal back and forth, making entries when it's your turn. And if the two live in different towns, that may be the only reasonable way to go about it.

An alternate method would be to have a joint journaling session every week or two, wherein each of you takes a turn writing in your mutual journal. Whichever way you plan to use, pick out the journal itself together, if possible. It'll feel like much more of a cooperative venture if you each have a voice in the decision.

The older person will probably take the lead in choosing the style and topic for the mutual journal. To maintain the child's initial interest, change the rules from time to time, working for a few weeks using one form, then switching to another.

You say the young'un is so into computers that he or she might shun the handwritten version? You can address this in one of two ways: You could create the whole thing on computer, mailing the jump drive back and forth and printing out a hard copy once a month or so; set up an intergenerational blog; or print out the computer entries and insert them into a hand-held journal.

The second version allows for writing shorter pieces and creating sketches directly into the book and adding computer printout pages as a companion method.

Here are a few ideas for entries:

> ‣ The high point of my week

- ▸ My favorite movie/TV show/fun activity lately
- ▸ What I saw on my walk outside
- ▸ My biggest problem at work/school this week
- ▸ One of my favorite exciting or laughing memories
- ▸ The neat new thing I tried doing

Encourage creativity by including some surprises like a silly poem you dreamed up about the child-journaler or a stick figure drawing of your neighbor's dog. A funny quotation or a made-up word might also stimulate them to try something new. But leave it up to them. You don't want your Mutual Journal to become a chore and a bore, or it'll die a quick and unlamented death. It should be mutually fun!

This Is Your Life!

Another option is to create a life journal for the youngster (or one for each of the children in your life). Like the infant's first baby book, this one will contain all the achievements and milestones of his or her life, with plenty of space for your own commentary about the event.

This also gives you a gilt-edged opportunity to share your deeper feelings about it, which is especially welcome for those adults who are uncomfortable expressing their emotions verbally. It's also a chance to tie these new events in with the rest of the family history. You'll find that even ten-year-olds like to reminisce about the high points of their lives.

You Got Your Driver's License!

Fri., Jan. 14th, 2000 – It's 3:30 pm on a sunny but cold day, and you just called to tell me you got your driver's

The Many Faces of Journaling

license! You had to retake the driving test because that dumb reduced-speed sign was blocked from your view by a tree. The policeman was really nice about it, but said since the sign was there, he had to take major points off your score.

But now you've got it! I'm so proud of you, Johnny. Here's a little family secret: my Dad was teaching me to drive when I was 15. I was having a really bad morning and told him I didn't think I should drive. He insisted I needed the practice, so of course we went. Unfortunately, my practice included driving into a brick retaining wall. (Those were the days of stick shift and no power steering, and since I felt sick, my reflexes were lousy!) He was angry and I was mortified. And I didn't have the courage to get behind the wheel again until I was 20.

I'm sitting here grinning at your accomplishment and discovered I'm already saying little prayers for your safety on the road. Nice going, John! (~Anonymous)

You can keep this journal for the full length of your life, or you can turn it over to the star of the book every five years or so and start a fresh one. I recommend the latter, because each shared "life journal" will create a fresh flush of love and mutual appreciation between the two of you.

Chapter 8

Historic Perspective Journaling

*History never looks like history when you are living through it.
It always looks confusing and messy,
and it always looks uncomfortable.*

— John W. Gardner

Most people feel very little connection to the kind of "history" that's published in textbooks. We read about wars and events, memorize names and dates, but have no real feel for how the typical man-on-the-street at the time viewed those same occurrences.

Personal Takes on Historical Events

Biographies do a better job of helping us live the moment, but they tend to be written by or about politicos and other public figures who still don't represent the folks next door. Colin Powell's *My American Journey: An Autobiography* (1995) takes a fascinating look at the Gulf War. But Powell doesn't pretend to represent

Everyman. Both our peers and our progeny can gain valuable insights by reading about the way that we experienced such historical events.

These two entries from Ralph Waldo Emerson's journals reflect his personal outlook on world and national events. The annexation of Texas precipitated the Mexican-American War:

March 1845 (age 41)

The annexation of Texas looks like one of those events which retard...the civilization of ages. But the World Spirit is a good swimmer, and storms and waves cannot easily drown him. He snaps his finger at laws.

(~ Ralph Waldo Emerson)

The next excerpt, also from Emerson, speaks of the early development of Chicago:

March 1865 (age 61)

Home from Chicago and Milwaukee. Chicago grows so fast that one ceases to respect civic growth; as if all these solid and stately squares which we are wont to see as the slow growth of a century had come to be done by machinery [the same way] as cloth and hardware are made, and were therefore shoddy architecture without honour.

(~ Ralph Waldo Emerson)

Such personal recordings help us with our own life perspectives. Do you remember the '70s as the "good old days?" Well how about the gas lines and crushing inflation? How did they affect your day-to-day decisions, your votes, and your peace of mind?

Where were you when the Challenger exploded? What were your first thoughts? Here's that entry from my journal:

The Many Faces of Journaling

January 28ᵗʰ, 1986

It was just a normal winter day. [After we'd painted our kitchen] I thought I'd damp mop the floor, scrub down cabinets, kick board, and the paneled walls. The launch of the Challenger had been delayed a couple of times – a door handle needed fixing and ice build-up had to be "knocked off."

The radio was on in the dining room & when I heard an "official confirmation" of something about Challenger, I charged into the dining room – Pinesol scrub cloth in my rubber gloved hands – curious whether they'd had to postpone the launch another day or not. What the woman announcer on KADI was telling us was that Challenger had exploded a little over a minute (74 seconds) after take-off! I ran to the TV trying to get CNN…In pained disbelief with tears streaming down my face, I watched an instant replay of the horrible catastrophe.

Like the day [President John] Kennedy was shot, I felt like a Divine covenant had been shattered. It was more than national pride & the fact that some things used to just be safe & sacred…these 7 astronauts, like President Kennedy, were our eager, bright, torch-bearers into the future. They were sacred in our mortal world and should have been safe – invincible.

Our journal entries can give those who come after us a far more realistic feel for the icy shock of death and disaster than any pallid textbook account ever can. We've shared the intimate reactions of the human heart.

The 1990 Gulf War has the honor of being the first television prime-time war in history. While civilian defense department employees were called upon to work lots of overtime, families watched the bombings in the comfort of their living rooms. It was both bizarre and obscene to flip back and forth between TV sitcoms and the war on any given night.

August 1990

What a very strange world we've become. Now we have a real live prime-time war. Let's see – how will the commentary go? Missile Scoreboard...Scuds 1, Patriots 2, pass the popcorn. For the very young, this is no more real than a video game. How awful for humanity!

I've often wondered how the families of the televised soldiers felt about the TV cameras. Then there was the reprise:

The Bombing of Baghdad

Wed., March 19th '03 – all day watching CNN & MSNBC. This evening the countdown on the latter. Right now it's 5 minutes and counting. Counting towards what? Armageddon? I'm starting to cry. This countdown isn't exactly like the New Year's Eve ball. But the reverse timing sounds & looks the same. Even that's obscene. Too much like a happy, hopeful, traditional annual event.

I cry – from fear. Fear of what exactly? Some of it is fear of war, that huge physical/psychological catastrophe. But I think I'm really more afraid of the massive, all pervasive, painful changes that have already begun in the world — that will surely intensify and find violent voice as each of our planes drops murdering bombs on innocent people. It's the awful, shameful backlash of hatred & utter distain from the rest of our fellow man.

I feel very young & helpless & vulnerable in ways that I don't even begin to understand. It's such a common

The Many Faces of Journaling

phrase – fear of unknown – it's so overwhelming, such a crushing feeling. The immediate future is suddenly scary and unknown, unstable, undependable.

"Opening stages of the disarmament of Iraq" – we've now begun bombing Baghdad. How very disingenuous of our media!! Early dawn in that capital, I can see an innocent softening of their morning sky on my TV. The bombing began about 1 ½ hrs. after deadline.

3 carriers involved in first small strike against Baghdad

Climax to the frenzied buildup. The feverish boil lanced.

"Decapitation attack" – aimed specifically at Saddam. How hideous

"Pax Americana" – said St. Louis journalist Ray Hartman. Peace indeed …

This is history in real life settings, and disasters can be far more appalling when they happen in the midst of domestic normalcy. You won't always be there to answer when youngsters ask such questions as where you were when Kennedy was shot, but that doesn't make your story any less important. *Write it in retrospect* if you weren't keeping a journal at the time.

November 22, 1963 - Friday

I remember it was a weekday. I was still living at home and was down in bed with some kind of flu bug. Mom and Mam were in the living room watching their soapies, when I heard a frightened exclamation (don't remember exactly what) from Mom. I called out to find out what was up, but nobody answered so I grabbed my pink robe and hustled in to join them. And there on the TV screen the stunned, ashen-faced veteran newscasters (I think it was Walter Cronkite) watched the studio clock, cupped hands around their ear pieces, and tried to provide a minute by minute update of the shooting, the drive to the hospital, and various reports on the President's condition.

The whole world was in a state of suspended animation as we listened and prayed and never once believed that our wonderful young president could possibly die.

Whon wo finally hcard the absolute, irrefutable announcement that his life was over, humanity shook its collective head in disbelief as tears flooded the land. He was dear to us and to our trust in a happy future in a way that many of us were unaware of until he was gone.

I for one had taken him and the Kennedy's "Camelot" completely for granted. I hadn't been a Kennedy groupie, but had taken his visions of the future as my own.

November 24, 1963 - Sunday

Jack Ruby shot Lee Harvey Oswald to death while I was teaching my Sunday School class of four year olds that they really shouldn't bite each other. The terrible sorrow of the time had finally reached a point where we were all kind of numb, shuffling around like red-eyed zombies.

Entertainment of the Times

Remember to include movies, popular entertainment, and sports in your entries. Here's a great bit of perspective from Walt Whitman written over a century-and-a-half ago. Notice this was written four months after the end of the Civil War:

The Many Faces of Journaling

August 1865

There was a big match played here yesterday between two base ball clubs, one from Philadelphia & the other a Washington club—& today another is to come off between a New York & the Philadelphia club I believe.

(~ Walt Whitman)

Statistics & Economics

Whether numbers are your thing or not, keeping a record of certain statistics paints an economic picture in and of itself. The average family's budget would include a list of household expenses: a loaf of bread, gallon of milk, gallon of gas at the pump, rent or mortgage payment, the price of a new car, and so forth.

Food

January 1989

per lb. of carrots – $.30
1 lb. canned tomatoes – $.55
1 lb. canned corn – $.40
frozen spinach (10 oz. pkg.) – $.53

November 1989

11 oz. salami – $3.00
7 oz. pkg. Gouda cheese – $2.60
Triscuits – $1.50 (about)

March 2008

per lb. of carrots – $.89
1 lb. canned tomatoes – $.67 (store brand)
frozen spinach (10 oz. pkg.) – $.99 (store brand)
12 oz. salami – $3.60
Triscuits – $3.19
Gallon of 2% milk (store brand, non-organic) – $3.93
Gallon of regular gas at the pump – $3.39

One of my old journal entries was entitled: Time Capsule. We lived in suburban St. Louis County (Missouri), and our son was just seven weeks old at the time.

Cost of Living

January 6, 1973...TIME CAPSULE: I spend about $22 a week for food—frugal but sufficient. [!] Whole chickens are twenty-five cents a pound, and it's no big deal to cut them up. I'm nursing the baby, and I use (and wash) cloth diapers except when we're away from home. My mom's cleaning woman charges $15 a day (about 6 hours). The load of topsoil for my new vegetable garden was $23.50, and the railroad ties were $3.75 each, delivered.

A partial list of the "big picture" prices and values might include stock markets at home and abroad; the price per troy ounce of gold; price per barrel of oil; and the relative values of the US dollar, British pound, German mark, Euro, and Japanese yen.

1974 Light Crude Oil —— $9.35 per barrel

October 12, 1990

DOW Jones Industrial Average — 2,398
Gold ———————— $388 per ounce
Light Crude Oil ————— $39.70 per barrel
British Pound ————— $1.96 US dollars

July 12, 1999

DOW Jones Industrial Average — 11.196
Gold ———————— $256 per ounce
Light Crude Oil ————— $19.74 per barrel
British Pound ————— $1.55 US dollars

As the United States has become more a part of the world economy, some of those statistics have changed dramatically. Granted, we are arguably in a recession, possibly inching toward stagflation. But the figures now have an even more powerful influence on our everyday lives, particularly in the area of oil.

April 7, 2008

DOW Jones Industrial Average —	12,639
NASDAQ —————	2,367
S&P 500 —————	1,374
Gold —————	$926 per ounce
Light Crude Oil ————	$109 per barrel
British Pound ————	$1.99 US dollars

Walt Whitman left a bit of pricing perspective from the Civil War period:

Strawberries of Yore

June 1863 We have strawberries good and plenty,15 cents a quart, with the hulls on—I go down to market sometimes of a morning and buy two or three quarts, for the folks I take my meals with.　　　(~ Walt Whitman)

By all means include a sampling of the jokes, political cartoons, popular songs, entertainers, games, and events of the day, for humor and amusement are as much a part of our history as disaster and economics. In order to make this kind of history journal really come alive, you'll want to include a wide assortment of elements that make up our lives.

The Many Faces of Journaling

Chapter 9

Environmental Journaling

*I think we're going to find, with climate change and everything else...
things like global warming and goodness knows what else and the cost of
fuel for a start...that things are going to become very complicated.[!]*

— *Prince Charles*

Whether you view the current fervor over global warming as circus
without substance or the biggest challenge to humanity since we
started walking upright, you know it's a white-hot topic (no pun
intended). The media's coverage of land, water, and air pollution
has long since moved into the big time.

There seems to be little ambivalence on the topic: few languish in
the gully of who-knows/I guess/maybe/we'll-see anymore. Now in
some social circles you can talk about religion, money, and sex,
but not about carbon footprints, or you could start a brawl!

From the local church to world governments to the huge International Panel on Climate Change, it's become as important to our

lives and futures as economic recession and the price of crude oil. Information of one sort of another comes at us from every news source and podium around the world. There's no escape. Pro or con, we're bound to think about it, and this is the ripe time to write out our thoughts and actions. Enter journaling. It's one more way to record your own version of current history.

Earth-Friendly Journaling

First, let's look briefly at the act of personal journaling from an environmentally responsible angle. There are a number of methods from which to choose:

- *Using Recycled Paper*: Buy journals made from recycled paper.
- *Going Paperless*: Try computer journaling.
- *Recording*: Create an audio journal using your personal recorder.
- *Blogging*: Start your own online, journal-style blog.
- *Photo Journaling*: Post your photos with captions on Flickr.com or a similar site.

As the range and capabilities of electronic gadgets expand, there will be ever more advanced ways of leaving a trail of your thoughts. Pick one or several of these alternatives to replace the traditional, leather-bound journal.

Like many blogs, mine (*aWritersRuminations.blogspot.com*) has a dual purpose: telling visitors about the life of a professional writer and teaching them about the business of writing and publishing. Here's an abbreviated version of one of the 2007 posts:

Cafe Writing

Fri., Nov. 16, 2007 – Yesterday morning, I met a book coaching client at the Pantera's, and for the next hour +, we analyzed and restructured the outline for Section II of her book. After she left, I got back to work on the environmental journaling chapter of MFJ2 [The Many Faces of Journaling 2nd Edition]. As happened at Kaldi's, I accomplished a great deal of writing (pen and legal pad) in just two, tightly focused hours. There were even a few quick sparks of inspiration! I love the way new surroundings stimulate new thoughts! And maybe the low pulse of conversation all around me boosts my "vibes," too. Much as I like my office, my brain gets a little stale looking at the same 4 walls day after day.

In photo journaling, some of the caption entries that go with the photos are funny, while others tell of background events, set the scene, or elaborate on the mood of the people shown thereon. You can even explain a long-running family tradition beside a photo of the event.

This kind of online photo journal never costs a tree to produce, unless the site's creator chooses to print a coffee-table color version of the pages. (*Those do make a lovely holiday gifts, by the way.*) Even so, the limited quantity would be fairly kind to our leafy friends.

My gifted photographer son, Kevin, has made great use of his Flickr.com site, posting family and artistic photos over the last few years. The written entry under each one is a story unto itself. Under an adorable picture of his 12-hour-old nephew (my grandson), Zander, Kevin wrote:

Eyes Wide Open

With his eyes wide open, his appetite sated and his sleep quota filled, Zander begins the lifelong process of answering the same question I ask every morning: What the Hell is going on around here and who are you people?

(~ Kevin T. Tisdel)

Your Thoughts on Environmental Issues

Accelerated deterioration of our planet's climatic stability and amazing break-through technologies can change the public's mood from one day to the next. Neither positive nor negative viewpoints tend to remain static.

Are you skeptical of all the hype, or is a visit to the recycling center part of your weekly routine? Chances are you lean in one direction or the other.

It does seem that more and more disposable products enter the marketplace every day, and that can light a fire under anyone concerned with the everlasting landfills of the world.

More Trashy Disposables!

I've done it again – talked back to the television. Correction – yelled at the television. These people, these corporations – are they so out of touch with the changing mood of this country and for that matter the world? Or is it the bottom line that drives so much of corporate America's decisions. A new product is now available which will add to the mountains of trash already inundating our environment. You now have the opportunity to scrub your potty, press a button and dispose of the brush-part in your plastic trash bag which will end up in the landfill where it will languish for eons! What a country!! So many of us are seriously working to come up with ways to reduce the amount of trash we generate daily and companies like this have the unmitigated gall to market another disposable product. Seems to me the old fashioned nondisposable potty brush works just fine thank you very much!!

(~ Vera Glick)

Then there are the more lethal forms of garbage.

Nuclear Disposables?

When will our lobbyist-swayed leaders stop this crap of burying toxic trash? How dumb - do they think as long as we can't see it, the environment'll be all safe and healthy?

And just how in hell do they figure nuclear is clean? Nuclear power plants... howz that for a fine solution to the fossil fuel depletion and carbon emissions dilemmas. Gee golly! Those spent [nuclear power plant] fuel rods only have a half life of hundreds of thousands of years, during which time the nuclear toxins can easily enter the soil and ground water – even if a quake or two doesn't speed up the process.

Are they all nuts? How about REALLY clean, like wind, solar and maybe hydroelectric power? Not enough pushy lobbyists to curry favor for those methods????

Not surprisingly, Beverly Letchworth, nature writer and author of *Leaf Bird Days & Firefly Nights*: *Personal Renewal through Nature Journaling*, has a keen interest in our climate.

April 22 ~ Green is Great!

As I put bird seed into the backyard feeder this morning I'm energized by the satisfying ambiance of green. Green grass, green bushes, green leaves on the trees. After a long gray winter, my soul rejoices at the many shades of green that surround me. I especially feel joy when I gaze at my beloved trees, now fully dressed and vitally active in growth and achievement.

I'm always awed by trees' accomplishments. They supply oxygen, use up carbon dioxide, dilute toxins and trap and filter out dust and pollen. They lower temperatures, increase humidity, slow down winds and act as sound barriers, plus they're pleasing to look at, and who can deny, a joy for children to climb and swing from.

When I consider all that trees do for us, I want to save as many as I can. That's why I'm happy about my decision to begin a new journal on my computer. For years I've kept a journal on paper, but because I feel I should do my part in improving our planet's environment, I want to reduce my consumption of paper and save a tree ... or two. If everyone saved a tree, how many million would be preserved to live and grow and perform their previous acts of restoration.

How appropriate that Green has become our Earth Friendly Motto.   (~ Beverly J. Letchworth)

Have your views on global warming and toxic landfills changed? On one hand, scientists regularly publish new evidence of mankind's contributions to earth's climate changes. On the other, some people think the whole thing has been blown out of proportion.

There's a Limit

I'm not sure how much of this is hype and how much is scientific fact. I mean, it's a huge leap from tracking air pollution to claiming we humans are actually affecting the polar ice cap! Haven't there always been climate cycles? I mean, what about the ice ages?

Maybe I should feel a little guilty when I throw bottles and cans in the trash instead of recycling. But who has time to mess with all that? Don't anybody tell me to get rid of my SUV or stop taking vacations. If electricity and gas keep going up, I'll turn the extra lights off to save my money. That's for real, not somebody else's fancy guesswork.

(~ Anonymous)

Local & Global Efforts to Curb Global Warming

From recycling church bulletins to China's ban on free plastic shopping bags, various communities, institutions, businesses, and countries have initiated changes to reduce our negative impact on the planet. Almost daily, the media announces new laws both local and international.

Environmental innovations crop up in both predictable and unexpected places. Heartening indeed was the announcement in January 2008 that University of Illinois's Champaign campus is constructing a "certifiably green" residence hall.

Go, U of I!

Be still my heart! U of I/Champaign's new dorm [Presby Hall] is leading the green campus parade. It's being built with geothermal heating, earth-friendly paint and lighting and special water-saving systems. Hey, maybe we should set up a big competition for the greenest campus in the land!!

(~ Ellie)

Individual responses to these mandates vary from enthusiasm to heated displeasure. Do you have any particular sticking points? Would you rather eat worms than pay for recycling pick-up? Or is your spirit willing, but circumstances impede your follow through?

Conserve it Forward

I keep hearing "Tell me one specific thing I can do or change that will really make a difference." Aaargh! Most of us will not make much impact through just one effort. It's going to take lots of little changes by lots of far-sighted people. Not only will that start to reduce pollution, but it will begin to turn the popular mindset around toward change.

If some people would just make one change a month, like recycling one more thing each month starting with cans, then trying to buy locally grown food, maybe plant a tree, buy recycled paper for the office or stop buying individually wrapped anything! I think a lot more people could move forward if they didn't try to do it all at once!

Personal Commentaries on News

We've been raised to judge virtually everything that crosses our paths, and there seems to be no end of annoying news about the environment – no matter which side of the debate you're on.

Can you read the newspapers or watch TV without talking back? Your journal is the perfect place to rant and rave and leave a legacy of your feelings at the same time.

Even a simple Sunday paper ad can produce an environmental response.

The Power of Ads

A new M&M's ad for Valentine's candy shows bright green M&Ms and says "Green is the new color of love!" Let's hear it for Madison Avenue!!!   (~ Ellie)

Obviously, nature writer Beverly Letchworth feels a powerful love of the earth and all the critters thereon. So it's hardly surprising that watching a couple of self-proclaimed experts blithely dismiss the evaluations of the international IPCC (Intergovernmental Panel on Climate Change) is enough to make her run to her computer journal to let off steam.

March 1st

I just heard a report on TV which has sent me to my computer again to vent my thoughts about whether or not our planet is in environmental trouble. Two, yes, they are scientists, scoffed at the dire predictions of catastrophe made by other experts in the field. Such predictions are exaggerated, they said, or will take centuries to come to pass.

Since I'm not an expert on these topics, I try to compile all the information I hear and use my common sense to evaluate them. And my common sense tells me that our planet is in trouble, and if we do not make drastic changes in our way of life, we will hasten the downfall of Earth. I'd rather err on the side of caution in this scenario. Maybe we won't suffer much from a deteriorating planet, but our children may and our grandchildren and great grandchildren definitely will.

Already global warming is altering environment. Pollution of air and water and habitat destruction have been rampant for decades and have caused an undetermined loss of animal and plant species. Who can deny that mankind has stamped its apathetic, irresponsible hand on the earth. But maybe it's not too late. Man has the intellect and compassion to solve problems. Man has the ability to heal if he puts his mind to it. But he has to start now before reversal is impossible. As always, this topic inspires passion. Unfortunately it depresses my mood as well. Remedy? I'm going to take a peek outside. Maybe the first crocus has broken ground. That touch of purple will revive my spirit. May new earthly life always be!

(~ Beverly J. Letchworth)

Our Grandchildren

I look at my 3 beautiful grandchildren: Caitlin Lizzie who is tall, slim and curious as a future scientist; Taylor, who is all boy and will one day be a man of compassion and laughter; and Zander who is the most precious little 14-month-old blonde bundle of love. I see them 25 years in the future. Will I then see in their eyes a Thank you, Nonni, for caring for our world. Or will there be looks of pain and love betrayed as they wonder how I could have cared so little for them, that I kept on destroying their earth long after we knew the consequences, until ultimately it was hardly more than a parched battleground. Please, God, let me make the effort to care for their future ...   (~ Nonni)

Environmental issues affect virtually every aspect of our lives. Our individual perceptions of the constant flood of new information and of steps taken and not taken will make for fascinating future reading for both the journaler and for generations to come.

Prince Charles' comment was prophetic – things already have become very complicated.

Chapter 10

Nature & Gardening Journaling

To see the World in a Grain of Sand
And a heaven in a Wild Flower,
Hold Infinity in the palm of your hand
And Eternity in an hour.

— William Blake

☙❧

Mother Nature offers us boundless resources for personal renewal. Who can crunch into a juicy Jonathan apple still warm from the tree, watch the antics of ducklings diving in a pond, or gaze at a bright rainbow without feeling a gentleness of the heart and a lift to the spirit? Journaling about nature lets you capture the moment and the emotion, so you can revisit it at will.

Backyard journaling may involve nothing more than observing the habits and interactions of the critters, feathered and furry, that visit your yard. Add to those the changes you see in the trees and other plantings, and you'll create a delightful record of the personalities and cycles of nature.

If you live in a high-rise apartment or condo, you can establish a miniature nature haven on your balcony or patio by installing a feeder or two, some plants, and a small improvised birdbath. (A saucer serves nicely.) Or you can make your observations in a nearby park or conservation area, revisiting the same place at various times to get a feel for Nature's rhythms and patterns.

Garden journaling involves keeping records of each season's planting layout, along with a list of the kinds planted and success rate for each one. In that way, you learn over the years which varieties of rose or rutabaga faired best in your climate and locale.

Backyard Journal

Record the various birds and critters that visit your backyard feeders, the butterflies that visit your flowers, the smell and feel of the changing seasons. Watch for the rituals and the family life of the feathered and the furry visitors and for changes in foliage, depending on the weather and seasonal change.

You'll enjoy this kind of journaling even more with the aid of a few props. First, a pair of binoculars will enable you to look at the bird hopping straight up the trunk of the shingle oak. With a visual assist, you can see that it wears a bright red cap atop its black and white body.

Next you'll want a small library of nature books. Start off with whichever topics most interest you. There are guides to birds, trees, wildflowers, animals, and edible wild plants. If you're an observer of the night skies, keep an astronomy volume handy, and consider buying a telescope for a more accurate study of the heavens. (Your bird book will identify the afore-mentioned red, black, and white bird as a downy woodpecker!)

Keep a dated log of all the creatures that come to your yard and feeders. On one special page—either the first or last page is quick to locate—simply list the various kinds of birds, butter-flies, and four-legged creatures. That'll give you a ready reference and an ongoing tally of the different species.

Some observations will lend themselves to sketching, either instead of or in addition to the "word pictures." These are purely for your own pleasure. Don't fret if they're not art gallery quality —that's not the point. You can add a rich dimension to your entries by including an assortment of colored pencils, an eraser, and a smudger to your journaling shelf. Art supply stores have a mind-boggling array of hues from which to choose. You may even want to start a sketch pad journal with the dates and locations noted at the bottom of each of your drawings.

Here are a few examples of neighborhood and backyard nature entries:

The first two are from the delightful *Leaf Bird Days & Firefly Nights: Personal Renewal through Nature Journaling* by Beverly J. Letchworth (2001):

Jack Frost Pastels

Stacking newspapers in the garage for a trip to the recycling center, I spy evidence that a famous visitor has made his appearance. Jack Frost has come and left one of his marvelous calling cards on the garage window. What an intricate pattern of swirls and squiggles frosted in white perfection on the glass! A skillful, delicate etching, making an ordinary window fit for royalty.

The snow is still with us. The teeming wildlife that over-whelmed summer is absent now. Some forms have died, of course. Some had migrated to warmer regions. But

The Many Faces of Journaling

countless others lie wrapped in cocoons or rest dormant and protected under brush, or hide away in burrows or dens to wait out the cold.

Looking at the snow-laden earth, I see a painting on canvas, static, lifeless. But Nature is there, waiting, even though we can't see it. Life lives. Reemergence will come.

(~ Beverly J. Letchworth)

Bits & Pieces

So much nature in May! Bits and pieces fill my journal this day. Blue jays remind me of spry little ladies with pointed bonnets, especially the fledglings.

Three young squirrels hop about the branches of the elm tree. Around and around the trunk they go, chasing each other. They seem to have accomplished all the proper moves already. Indeed, they have to if they are to survive.

Fledgling house sparrows beg for food from their parents. If the young didn't make such a commotion with their fluttery wing movements, you couldn't tell they were young birds, for they're the same size as the adults. Of course they are. They've been lounging in the nest all their lives being fed.

A downy woodpecker on the elm, two rabbits under the pine.

(~ Beverly J. Letchworth)

The next is a simple entry from Ralph Waldo Emerson's journal:

March 1861 (age 52)

I hear this morning, whilst it is snowing fast, the chickadee singing.   (~ Ralph Waldo Emerson)

These squirrel observations are taken from my journal.

Milton the Nest Maker

Jan. 31, 1989…Our crazy little friend Milton Squirrel has been trying to build a nest on our windowsill. I've watched him gnaw off small branches of the evergreen, one at a time, and leap over to the sill with the branch still in his mouth. He'll get three or four stacked up, then begin this super-efficient looking dance. I'm thinking to myself – So, that's how they do it! – Fascinating…They just sort of weave the twigs together with a lot of clever twitching of their paws and a little squirrelly hocus-pocus.

And, old Milton, well you can tell by the tilt of his head, he's thinking "Damn! I'm good!!" Only, bless his heart, he really isn't, and pretty soon the branches tumble over the edge of the sill. The silly little beast leans over and peers down at the ground below the window, seems to shrug and goes bounding off into the trees. I swear to you, there is quite a stack of Milton's twigs piled up on the ground.

Some Nuts Are Just Different

Feb. 3, 1989…Milton doesn't care for almonds. I brought a clam shell up from the patio because it's rough-bottomed and won't slide off the window sill so easily. Now every morning I raid the nut bowl on the coffee table and place two [unshelled] nuts in the clam dish. Yesterday the menu included an almond and a pecan. Little Milton is a curious soul, and went for that strange nut right off the bat. He nibbled and ptooey-ed the pithy shell until he came to the meat. One small bite of the almond and friend squirrel politely set it back down on the sill, turned and grabbed up the pecan and went bounding away into the tree. He came back a little later and took a nap a few inches away from the abandoned almond, but he never paid any more attention to it. So I guess the squirrelly moral is...all nuts are not alike. At least according to Milton.

Out & About

Local parks and neighborhood walks reveal scads of nature's small miracles. Perhaps you'll choose to record the life cycle and idiosyncrasies of the duck and goose families. Or make a sketch journal of the trees and flowers, and jot down notes on your obser- vations of fauna and flora—feathered, footed, and otherwise.

Our seasonal changes in the Midwest produce marked shifts in color, sound, smell, and texture. The next two entries reflect summer and fall in or around St. Louis. Journal entries become far more interesting when you incorporate the sense of touch, smell, and sound as well as sight into your writing, whether you plan to share your journals or keep them for your personal pleasure.

Some outdoor situations lend themselves to poetry in one form or another. This entry was written in the car on the way back to St. Louis, Missouri from Michigan.

Steamy Illusion

It's Army convoys, tiger lilies,
Reed-rimmed stock ponds,
RV's with skiffs wagging
Merrily behind.

It's cold beer, sticky street tar,
RBIs, Feathers flapping
In a communal dustbath.

The Many Faces of Journaling

It's the sweet seductive scent of mock orange,
Hickory smoke,
Sour towels, Roman candles,
Snap beans and pickled cukes,
The muggy illusion of leisure
We call summer.

The spectacular colors and textures of a Midwest autumn seldom fail to stir the soul. This entry, which began with a long look out of the window, evoked memories of the winter before and conjecture for the one ahead.

Autumn in Kirkwood

Oct. 28, 1999...Ah, the sweet gum tree across the street from my office window invited me out for a walk today. It's a gorgeous combination of glowing shrimp- and lemon-colored leaves, and I know there are more like it around the neighborhood. What is it about dry autumn leaves? It's not just the crunchy walking and the woodsy smell, it's everything. All my senses feel the earth in the fall. I have this intense desire to flop down and roll around on the ground, and just play with the earth. (So far I've restrained myself!) Today as I walked down to the old train station, I spotted a warm green leathery leaf on the sidewalk – it seemed to want me to pick it up, so I did. And brought it home to press in the old phone book. One more special dried leaf to decorate my bulletin board!

The nip in the air makes me wonder how long we have to wait for our first snow. Last year either El Nino or Global Warming did a number on our winter weather, and the only snow we got was that awful ice and snow combination around New Years. That was no fun! It was too slippery to even get down the front steps! I want to walk down to

The Many Faces of Journaling

Starbuck's catching snowflakes on my tongue as I go.
Come on, snow!

If you enjoy scouring the countryside for wild edibles like morel
mushrooms, persimmons, hickory nuts, and other delicious
treasures of nature, keep a log of when and where you find the
most productive sites. You may have to make some rough sketches
so you can find the specific hillside or tree again next year.

Take your wild edibles book along when you go hiking, and don't
just look at the pictures. Read the information about each plant
you're tempted to eat. Many are safe and tasty when they're very
young, but can be bitter and even toxic when they reach a certain
size. Others you'll learn to identify as poisonous at all stages of
growth.

A Gardening Journal

This kind of log lets you keep track, year by year, of the plantings,
prunings, and problems that you encounter in your own little
corner of the natural world. Be it vegetable gardens, flower beds,
trees shrubs, or lawns, there's regular information to be recorded.

Keep a chart of the bulbs and tubers and the dates on which you
divide them. Note when and where you first noticed the infesta-
tion of tent worms, how you treated them, and what seemed to
work the best to eradicate the pests. It's easy to lose track when life
gets busy!

If you keep a chart of your vegetable garden each season, you
won't replant the same crop in the same place every year (a
practice that can encourage certain plant-specific insect invasions)
or repurchase the variety that wilted in your climate. It also allows
you to build upon what you learn, instead of having to relearn the
same lessons year after year.

The Many Faces of Journaling

When you sketch out your **garden plan**, include companion plantings like nasturtiums and marigolds that act as natural insect repellents. Mark the location of your cucurbits (the gourd family that includes cucumbers, squash, and melons) and other plant families so you can rotate them to a different part of the garden every year. That simple step can go a long way towards reducing insect infestations. Illustration #2 shows a basic garden plan.

On a page just before or after the layout sketch, list the plants and varieties, planting date, and the dates of the first and last harvests. You can also note the times and types of fertilizer, insecticide, or other plant treatments and their effectiveness.

Make note of any way the plant's growth and progress differs from the ad copy (e.g., tomatoes were smaller, lettuce heads grew larger, this variety was subject to mildew on the leaves, etc.). Write out a description of any insect pests, birds, or animals, which plants they were attracted to, and how you dealt with the problem.

Your yard journal might also contain a pruning and spraying schedule. This is especially useful if you have fruit and nut trees. Note the times and weather conditions of each pruning and chemical application, and compare results at the end of each growing season. Be sure to include notes on the size and condition of the harvest.

Although not gardening information, this is a good place to record termite and other insect inspections and treatments.

Nature has a wonderful way of grounding us and helping us keep life in perspective. Writing in a nature journal not only allows us to enjoy the outdoors over and over again in the rereading, it helps

Basic Garden Plan

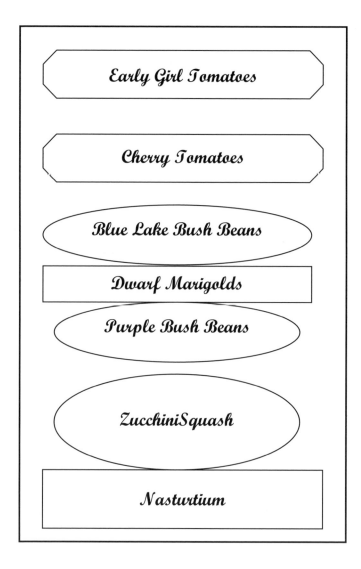

Early Girl Tomatoes

Cherry Tomatoes

Blue Lake Bush Beans

Dwarf Marigolds

Purple Bush Beans

ZucchiniSquash

Nasturtium

Illustration #2
Backyard Garden 1986

The Many Faces of Journaling

open our eyes to the fascinating world of critters and flowers and bushes and things.

Whether you decide to keep a nature and/or gardening journal, or simply make such notes in a general chronological journal, jot down the fascinating little tidbits of nature trivia that pop up from time to time through radio, television, and reading rather than direct observation. I discovered a few gems in the course of researching an article a few years ago.

Bees

‣ Honeybees have short tongues which can't reach all the way to the nectar in deep blossoms.

‣ Bumblebees and butterflies have longer tongues.

‣ Bees look for nectar blossoms in the full sunshine.

‣ Bees like large groupings or bunches of flowered plantings, and are particularly attracted to bright colors.

Weather

Weather is another aspect of nature that often has a major impact on our lives. Whether it's monsoons, tornadoes, record snow-storms, drought, or temperature extremes, these forces of nature can affect our homes, yards, vacations, and a whole host of other events.

When did we have that horrible hailstorm—the one that smashed the living room windows and storm door? A note in either your nature or chronological journal will tell you. *Is it time to water the*

garden yet? Look in your log to see on what day you had the 2"
rainstorm. It's also fun to make note of the extremes, such as heavy
rains, snowfalls, heat, or cold.

Many journalers include extreme or especially destructive natural
disasters around the world. Occasionally noting such events can
put your own rainstorms in perspective.

There are virtually no limits to the rich variety of information you
might include in your nature journaling. Experiment. Go on a one-
month quest for new and fascinating nature facts and personal
observations. Your entries will be even more fun to read next year
than they are to record now.

Chapter 11

Dream Journals

*Dreams and beasts are two keys
by which we find out the
keys of our own nature.*

— *Ralph Waldo Emerson*

Our dreams can be a gloriously rich source of entertainment and wisdom! Through the act of journaling our dreams, we can learn about our past and present joys, longings, fears, attitudes, and delights. Making regular entries in a dream journal will create a unique tool for deeply personal enlightenment.

Remembering Dreams

Some people claim they never remember their dreams and still others even doubt that any occur. Others discount dream content as simply being so much garbage coughed up by the sleeper's subconscious and, therefore, of no earthly significance. Those of us who have learned and benefited from our dreams vehemently disagree. Our nocturnal revelations, if heeded, analyzed, and recorded, often lead us to growth and healing that can find no other way into our conscious thought.

Boosting Dream Recall

Here are a couple of time-honored techniques to help increase your recall:

#1 – When you go to bed at night, have a short chat with your subconscious. Tell it that you value your dreams and truly want to remember them. Ask for help in doing so. No matter what you think of that approach, you're reinforcing the desire to remember.

#2 – The other method is to jot down a few fragment words when you awaken from the dream. Waiting until morning can be a huge mistake. The dream that felt so emotionally powerful can disappear forever with the morning dew. Even more frustrating is a freeze-frame glimpse of the dream, which you're unable to connect with the full sequence or the message therein.

Also beware of processing the dream as soon as you awaken from it during the night as a substitute for jotting those few key words down. I've done some very insightful mental dream analysis at three o'clock in the morning, positive that such ruminations would imprint the dream so I could readily recall it the next day, only to find all traces of it gone with the sunrise.

Buy a ballpoint pen with a light in the tip (you twist the cap to turn it on), and keep that and a notepad on your bedside table. Just a few words jotted on the pad can bring the dream back to you the next day in all its glory. Some people favor a bedside tape recorder for this purpose; others find that too noisy and complex for middle-of-the-night use.

Writing dreams out in full detail can be so time consuming that you may feel disinclined to spend so much time on them. For some of us, computer writing is much faster and allows us to come closer to stream-of-consciousness recall. When writing them out longhand, use abbreviations; leave out obvious words; and ignore style, form, and grammar. Those niceties are irrelevant here. If you're in a rush, just write two or three sentences, adding more at your leisure. Anything you can do to capture even a portion of the dream will help.

Dreaming in Metaphors

They come in several flavors, dreams do, and you may not understand the message until you actually record the dream. Such was the case in this one. The analogy popped up in the process of dream journaling.

They were shooting me down...

As first I thought this was one of my Hollywood-type, purely-for-entertainment dreams. It looked like a combination of a desert war and Star Wars scene. I was in the open side-door of a helicopter, holding on to both sides, with the swirling sand blowing in my face as we lifted off.

The helicopter was approaching a kind of farmer's hut or small adobe dwelling (I told you it was like Star Wars!) where my in-laws lived. Then I saw them both at the front window with shot guns pointed up at me, blasting away. At first I thought they were firing around me so I could land safely. Then I realized they were firing right at me! Then it occurred to me. This dream symbolized my in-laws always trying to shoot me down! Pretty damned accurate.

Changes in our lives, both large and small, often stimulate active dreaming. While we're in the throes of learning and growing, we're often too closely involved to see how extensive the accompanying internal changes may be. The dream-self offers a slightly different, expanded view if we're able to take time to record the dreams when they're fresh.

The way the subconscious mind chooses to send its messages is often wonderfully inventive. Have you ever noticed that in the process of writing out a dream journal entry the real message of the dream is contained in a metaphor? You could almost put these revelations in a smiler journal, for they tend to elicit an "Aha!" of surprise and appreciation. Here are a couple of prime examples:

You're going to get burned!

Good grief! Now my subconscious is getting preachy! Here's the dream I had in the early hours of this morning. (I might add this was after spending a lot of time before I went to sleep last night thinking wonderful, tingly thoughts about you-know-who, which can't ever happen, cause he's just as married as he was when I first met him!)

There were 2 wood-burning stoves 6 or 8 feet apart. The front doors of both of them were open, and were full of hot, burning-glowing logs. I was trying to transfer the coals from the stove on the left to the one on the right using only a pair of log tongs (not very good ones, either). I was working hard/not accomplishing much, plus I knew it was dangerous and I could get badly burned.

After I woke up, I thought about what a weird dream it was, and talked my way back through it. My big clue? "You're playing with fire!" obviously referring to my fantasies about Mr. Tingles. Just what I need – a smart-ass dream!!!

(~ Anonymous)

At the time of the next dream, I had embarked upon a period of spiritual exploration. It proved to be a time of rich personal discovery, but for a time the input was too constant and all-encompassing to allow for perspective. The subconscious stepped up to offer this insight.

White Horses

I had bought 4 rather wonderful white plow horses (dappled with very light gray spots), w/leather harnesses to help in the work I was doing (whatever that was?!). Bought them off the street from 2 or 3 different people. Then we were going to move to another town, and there was no place for the horses there, but I didn't know how to get rid of them.

I kept trying to find out what to do with the horses. Searched the Yellow Pages and tried calling to find a place for them. Somebody asked us where we were moving…maybe we could just keep the horses. But I said, oh no, we've moving to Nevada…I envisioned a map when I said this and "Nevada" was a small town not too far west of St. Louis. But there was no more need for the horses, even though they still looked wonderful with their gentle brown eyes.

I'd outgrown my need for them in some way. I don't know why the quandary over what to do with them. But nobody seemed to want to buy them, or need them either. I guess they've just outlived their usefulness, but were still dear creatures.

I wonder if this has anything to do with my spiritual growth, and the final casting away of old frameworks of black & white shoulds and definitions. I really don't know. Maybe I'll see if I can get a clarification of the dream tonight.

Mary Stuart says, "Jung believes that the archetype of dogs represents the messenger (i.e., if you dream of dogs, your unconscious is trying to send a message to your conscious self)." This is her "messenger dream" entry:

Undated

My dream takes place in my own house where I've lived only a short time after spending a year and a half hiding out in a rented apartment surviving a devastating divorce. I hear barking in the neighborhood and [my dog] takes up the hue and cry and stands tail up at the back door barking like crazy. Pretty soon I notice there are at least 20 or 30 dogs running around in the neighborhood behind my house, with two postal deliverymen hiding in the bushes. When I open the door to look out, my dog runs out to join the fray and pretty soon I have dogs everywhere...in my house, running in and out of my house, in my backyard, all of them making quite a ruckus, but in a happy joyful way.

On waking, I realize that although I had not wanted to be divorced I had nevertheless lost my voice in the marriage, along with large pieces of myself, and the dogs jumping and barking and playing were reflective of my new, more hopeful outlook on my life and myself.   (~ Mary Stuart

Paths to the Subconscious

Some dreams lead to useful breakthroughs in therapy. You can tell by the tone that the following was a very "heavy" dream, but it proved effective in unearthing some corrosive, deeply buried emotional issues.

Monster Dad

Fall - I don't even want to remember this dream but I know it's important. It's about my dad, and in this dream he's

The Many Faces of Journaling

kind of a monster. We (dad, me, little girl whom I believe to be Little Me, and in the background other little girls – more little me's? – mom and grandma, and it seems like a few other unidentified people) we're at somebody's house I think – there are people in many different rooms.

The beginning is a little foggy, but it seems like one after another of the people suddenly became stricken by some mysterious bad thing. The best symptom I can remember was that a place on the person's face started deteriorating sort of like a beginning patch of a flesh-eating virus. We didn't know what caused it, but everybody (I think "everybody" was female) was really scared.

Somehow I discovered (from sleuthing/digging, I think) that my dad was causing this. He'd just touch a girl on the cheek and she was stricken. (All he had to do was touch her face with his fingers/hand.)

Anyway, once I figured it out, the next time he came in a room, I confronted him, and disabled his bad abilities. And told him he couldn't do that anymore. Made some kind of threat, I think, but that was basically it.

I was so scared by the dream, the mysterious awful menace, the fear of my dad, the evil look on his face, that it took a while for me to remember that I'd successfully confronted and stopped him. So I should have felt good and powerful, but I didn't. I felt lousy.   (~ Anonymous)

Revelations

Dreams often furnish us with wake-up calls direct from the dreamer's subconscious, realistically identifying those negative feelings we try to ignore or deny in the light of day. If we listen to

The Many Faces of Journaling

the dream messages and apply those personal insights to our everyday reactions, we often wind up feeling a lot less put-upon.

Taking Advantage

In this dream I was loading up the car, leaving some kind of church or similar event, and issued a "Can I give anybody a lift?" invitation. This woman whom I didn't really know, said Oh, Yes! and instantly plopped herself in the back seat. I asked which direction she lived – she said west. Then she said Oh, I need to get my "cake pan"…this was an oddly shaped very long, maybe 6 foot long metal pan.

I asked her how she'd gotten to the event, and she said she and her husband had come together, but the pan wouldn't fit into the car going home. (?) The husband was driving away at that point. I'm beginning to feel a little put upon. I had to lower seat backs and clear out the trunk and do all kinds of work to accommodate her – going a lot more out of my way, figuring out solutions that I hadn't known before, than I'd intended when I asked if anybody wanted a ride. I felt she was taking advantage of me, but didn't want to go back on my offer.

We started out, got to the first stop sign, and I said Just exactly where do you live anyway? She replied – Chesterfield – a suburb approximately 45 minutes from where we were. At that I'd had enough. This woman I'd barely met (didn't know her name, nor she mine), was taking advantage of my good nature and I'd finally hit my limit. I said OK, that's it. I'll take you as far as (some intersection) and you can get your husband to pick you up from there. I was really steamed.

> As I played around with the phrases "took advantage
> of my offer," "abused my good will," "pushing me farther
> and farther," and "finally had enough," I realized how
> this paralleled a situation in my life where somebody I
> thought I knew, but evidently didn't took horrible
> advantage of me until I finally said "Enough!" The dream
> showed me how my intentions started out fine, and how
> slow I was to actually pull the plug. Makes me feel a
> whole lot better that I did!   (~ Anonymous)

Some dreams are insightful and help us sort through the dilemmas of our business, social, or emotional lives. Others celebrate our progress in improving outlook and developing a positive sense of self.

When we record the dreams, we can better understand what aspects of our lives have contributed to the change in a dream pattern, showing us that we're on the right (or wrong) track.

Recurring Dreams

It's common to keep experiencing the same dream over and over for a period of years. These often have a negative tone such as fear, dread, or frustration of some kind. Journaling these can help us track and learn from their evolution. The act of writing them out also helps us to feel a little less at the mercy of the dreams.

Such was the evolution of this dream pattern. It seems to be proof-positive that certain deliberate changes in daily living were having a wonderfully upbeat effect on the writer's sense of personal security. First, the original dream, which had been recurring for over two decades:

The Apartment

1999…It was back again last night. For years and years, through my painful marriage whenever I felt like I had to escape, I've dreamed that I went back to "my apartment." It isn't literally the same place I lived before I was married, but symbolically it's a place of refuge where I can just be me. Again I was blocked. First I couldn't remember which street it was on, then couldn't remember which building it was. I tried to bluff my way through, hoping to find some recognizable sign or landmark, knowing I was in the right section of town by the old red of the brick buildings – all the while denying how disoriented I felt. Got inside and didn't recognize anything from the apartment floor and number to the mailbox number to the color of the exterior! People were coming and going mostly in small congenial groups, and I was out of place and couldn't get in.

That always leaves me feeling sad – the little kid with her nose pressed again the window – on the outside looking in, thinking I used to belong here. So today I felt crummy pretty much all day.   (~ Anonymous)

After many years of endless variations of the "can't go back" version of this dream, a breakthrough occurred for this dreamer. By recording it in full and dating it, the writer could see how recent changes in her life had come to alter her internal attitude.

The New & Improved Apartment!

I can't believe it! What a terrific change – I swear I woke up grinning. I dreamed I went back to "my apartment" after having been gone for a long time. I didn't doubt that I was in the right place, although I still wasn't sure about the mailbox number. My family was with me – Dad, Mom, Gram, I don't know who all, and when I/we walked in the

front door the apartment manager greeted me like a long
lost friend (in a kind of reserved, gruff-guy way). He said
something like We've missed seeing you – where have
you been? Something like that. No hugs, just a really
sincere welcome.

I saw that a couple of twenty-something guys were living in
my old apartment (it was a dream – there were no walls). I
figured that meant I was out of luck, but the manager said
Hey would you like to move back? I can find another place
for these guys to stay.

And he handed me my back mail and seemed to really
hope I'd be moving back. Wow! What a change on my old
dream! Now I feel wanted and included and all that...all
positive stuff. Hurray!   (~Anonymous)

Our dreams can enlighten, entertain, puzzle, and heal us. Entering
them in a dream journal allows us to build a useful connection to
the many aspects of the subconscious, which speak to us through
our dreams.

The Many Faces of Journaling

Chapter 12

Chronological Journaling

*Life must be lived forwards,
but can only be understood backwards.*

— *Soren Kierkegaard*

For many of us, recording the happenings and observations of our lives in chronological order is the most comfortable journaling method because it's familiar. Our diaries from childhood on through adulthood started with January 1 and went on through the year. Publishers often use the one-page-a-day layout for the journals we see on the bookstore and stationery shops' shelves. (That style has always annoyed me because on one hand, there may not be enough room for all I have to write; on the other, the blank unfilled pages are a nagging reminder of absent entries.)

For that reason, I urge you to select one that doesn't have the date marked at the top of each page (or ignore the printed date) if you decide to use one book for all of your journaling. An unlined journal will appeal more to those who want to include art work,

The Many Faces of Journaling

and the blank pages seem to give you permission to write huge, crooked, rambling entries if you're so inclined. If you shop for a lined book, be sure you're comfortable with the spacing provided. Wide spacing won't appeal to those who have tidy handwriting, and narrow spacing brings out the rebel in a free-style writer. A 9 ½ " x 6" spiral-bound notebook makes a useful family journal. Keep it near the telephone, and fill in specific events before or when they occur. I used facing pages for each one-week period as shown on the examples on pages 148 and 149.

Notice how this example serves multiple functions as a date book, menu planner, birthday reminder, auto maintenance record, health chart (blood pressure medicine and weight), weather record, and gardening planner all in one tidy volume. I always favored the five-sections size with one section for each year.

Chronological entries work particularly well for both children and adults who are going through a time of transition, because the layout invites then-and-now comparisons. In Chapter 3, *Therapeutic Journaling*, we talked about the cathartic value of writing your way through a life-changing event like marriage, divorce, a new job, or the death of a loved one. That allows you to ventilate the monstrous fears, shaky dreams, and uncertainties involved in major life-shifts.

But most of our weeks consist of mundane, everyday happenings, the journaling of which provides a valuable record of progress during the non-crisis times, which comprise our days. Writing your daily or weekly entries creates a life overview. When you can see the juxtaposition of your child's bike accident, the scary rumor about your company downsizing, and the flood waters that crept all the way up to the electrical outlets in your basement, you can understand why you felt like you were losing your mind around that time!

Pain & Healing

Anne Morrow Lindbergh, wife of aviation hero Charles A. Lindbergh, Jr., wrote these painful entries after the death of her beloved sister, Elisabeth:

Wednesday, December 12, 1934

...what I must work out is my life without her, going on without her...I must be what I was with her, for, as always and with everyone she touched, the truest clearest person came out at her touch. She had the gift of clarifying you, a creative sympathy.   (~ Anne Morrow Lindbergh)

Sunday, March 17, 1935 [Elisabeth's birthday]

A tearing wind, but still bright. I put flowers on Elisabeth's grave...I do not and cannot think of that copper vault as holding Elisabeth. The flowers, though, look like her, freesia, tulips, iris, mimosa, daffodils–very gay–and I pick some pale blue crocuses from the garden.

(~ Anne Morrow Lindbergh)

This entry from a few months later indicates that she is emerging from her grief.

Monday, July 15, 1935

I feel marvelously released this morning, calm and controlled...The mist has come in, shutting me in, thrusting me back on myself. The mist is cooling too. To have the world drenched in it is a relief.

(~ Anne Morrow Lindbergh)

Sample family journal pages –
left page (facing right page)

Planted tomatoes, peppers ^ zuc	Sun
	Mon
Got replacement processor from Brothers	Tues
	Wed
	Thurs
	Fri
Kev teaches 9:00-11:30	Sat
Antipasto salad: rst. Beef	
Salami	
tomatoes	
Cooked gr. beans	
Sweet peper	
Olive & feta	

Sample family journal pages –
right page(facing left page)

June	
7	Brats & kraut/boiled po /Smiths here for dinner
8	Chicken/gr. beans & po
9	Taco salad /me – dentist – 10:30
10	Cold chick/corn/ tomatoes
11	Fish/grits/ beets & slaw /John – church mtg.
12	Pot roast w/carrots & po /movie
13	Pizza /Little Jen here overnite
	REMEMBER – Mom's b-day the 18th!!!

Childhood

All occurrences in the early years of our lives seem vitally important at the time. Our lack of life experience elevates every new event to an exalted status. In the course of writing this book, I unearthed my diary from junior high. What a revelation!

First, the diary itself is vintage '50s. It's about 4½" x 5¾" with a cartoon drawing of two teenage sweethearts on the blue leatherette cover, and it has a lock that any moron could pick open with a hairpin. It's a compact little brick of diary pages. For those of you with long memories, it was a genuine Betty Betz Five-Year Diary.

Decades have passed since I last opened it, and the entries reveal a young woman-child filled with romantic dreams, family vacations, school, and some surprisingly honest comments. One February I wrote, "I stayed home though I should have gone"—to school, that is. I wasn't above faking to be able to goof off for one more day.

Two years later, in 1957, I wrote about my first Missouri State DeMolay Grand Ball at the Moolah Shrine Temple in downtown St. Louis. I had just turned fifteen, and had met a "doll-l-l" of a guy at the informal get-together the night before the big shindig. That was one of a very few mixers that had a thoroughly happy outcome for me. Names have been changed out of deference to middle-age sensibilities.

July 27, 1957 - Saturday

Danny and Tommy met us on the sidewalk of the temple and we sat where we had the previous eve. They got each of us lovely (unexpected!) wrist corsages of white pompom mums…Tommy said he wished there was somewhere we could go but there wasn't so-o-o. He kissed my hair, ear, cheek, and nose, but it was rather a public place for a real kiss!

Encourage your young friends and family members to keep their diaries or journals. The trials and euphoria of youth are so easily lost in memory. Only the youth's words written at the time of the events will capture the emotional essence of the moment.

Timeline Perspective

Chronological journaling offers us a truly unique overview of our own lives and changing perspectives. An entry fifteen years later than the above entry illustrates how your focus can change as a thirty-year-old wife with an 18-month-old daughter and newborn son.

July 27, 1972

Vera here for coffee [with her infant son Jeff]. Dyed bathroom rugs purple. Tried Kev on oatmeal again. Can't really be sure. [Which was shorthand for "this may or may <u>not</u> be one of the allergens that cause him such intestinal distress."]

Thirteen years later, with both kids approaching orthodontia and the family budget yelping every time I opened the checkbook, dollar-stretching often showed up in the journal:

August 16, 1985

I'm doing pretty well on the temporary food budget cutback. The check made out for cash [for groceries] are only about $15 less per [biweekly] pay period than they used to be, but out of that food money I've bought cigarettes, wine, small toiletries, and miscellaneous items so they wouldn't add to the Mastercard bill. For dinner tonight we had jungle omelet: 4 strips of bacon + potatoes + 9 eggs (very economical with the eggs on sale), hot French bread (day old bread store 60¢) and mixed on-hand-fruit salad.

The Many Faces of Journaling

Five years later the world and I experienced many changes:

August 30, 1990

So much has happened in the world and within our family!
[It wasn't unusual for me to play catch-up after neglecting
the journal for a while.] As of Aug. 20th when we drove
away from Columbia, our household is just [my husband]
and me again after nearly 20 years of parenting. Both kids
are now in college.

In the world, Iraq and the US + other UN forces continue
their desert standoff. The first newscast of the morning is
an adventure, partly because the day is more than half
over in Europe and the Middle East...Instead of my usual
radio listening, I'm glued to CNN at lunch time...My writing
is utterly without direction at the moment and somehow I
must come up with another project.

Reading back over years of accumulated journals can provide a life
perspective that's unavailable in any other way. When your family
talks about these events, the stories relate their perceptions of what
happened, which may be quite different from the way you experienced the situation. Family pictures may evoke memories of events
and family happenings, but won't reflect your small, daily
achievements and concerns.

Such a view of your growth is valuable whatever your age. Chronological journaling allows you to read back over the anticipation,
the reality, and the response. Those of us who have moved from
our parents' house to a home of our very own will relate to these
entries.

Getting My First Apartment

I figured I would write about it now before all the jittery
newness wore right off of it, but this will most likely be the

last week I spend living under the same roof as my parents for the rest of my life. I sign the lease on my new apartment Monday at 4:00 pm. This will be my first time living entirely on my own. I mean, I moved out before but I was living with my friend Marcia, at least I had a caring face to come home to. This time will be totally different. I think living alone will get old very quickly. I have this funny feeling that one day I will read this journal entry and laugh at the dwarf I used to be. Maybe now I am just dazzled at the thought of the giant I will be then. That probably doesn't make any sense to you. I am really tired.

(~ Mindy Gramling-Bailey)

A short time later she wrote this about the adjustment of living alone.

In My First Apartment

The new apartment is finally unpacked. It's going well. Coming home to loose space is getting easier. At least for this week. A couple more days and who knows where thoughts will take me? I need a stepladder. I keep forgetting to buy one.   (~ Mindy Gramling-Bailey)

Octogenarian May Sarton, prolific and gifted poet, novelist, and journal writer, found perspective in reading over past entries, as this one shows:

Tuesday, May 17, 1994 (age 82)

I have been reading my journal, in the last two months anyway—that is, March and April—and it has been a painful experience because it is a description of severe depression…So even though I [still] feel quite ill, I keep telling myself, "In a month you will feel a lot better, and won't it be wonderful if Prozac works?"   (~ May Sarton

By the same token, reflecting back on the supremely confident entries of our unseasoned youth can offer great insights into the adult that emerged from that innocence.

August 8, 2000 - 12:01 p.m.

I'm reading through my journals from a decade ago. (Shudder.) I wonder if the word "journal" has the same origins as the word "journey." It's been quite a journey from age 20 to age 30! College days...full of angst, uncertainty, discovery, questioning. There are passionate, sometimes irate entries about devastating conflicts with people I don't even REMEMBER now. Hindsight is so 20/20. My awkward attempts to make sense of things and to get the perspective and mental clarity that I so wanted remind me in retrospect of a gerbil on an exercise wheel.

And yet, despite the cycles of learning, forgetting, relearning, forgetting, relearning again, etc., I am happy with where I am now. No longer insecure, self-doubting, overly sensitive, out of balance; I no longer "sweat the small stuff," and I understand concepts of power, dignity, and integrity that I didn't even know to explore a decade ago. This is what Mom calls an "atta girl" moment. Having become a content, balanced, loving woman was no accident. It's the result of hard and humbling work on myself. ATTA GIRL, "h"!   (heather)

August 8, 2000 - 3:17 p.m.

I have many journals filled with pain, struggle, and emotional turmoil. The entries are an unsettling, nauseating trip back in time to degrading, humiliating experiences that are thankfully behind me. They remind me of my youthful inability (unbeknownst to me at the time) to foresee consequences, to assert myself, and to demand to be treated with dignity by others. Looking through these books is like peeking in the windows of an old building in a "bad" part of town, with rotting floors, bullet hole-pocked walls, and a pungent stench.

But the foundation of this collapsing building is still good. How exciting to burn it down to the foundation and build it up again, intact and sturdy, clean and bright. Urban renewal on a personal level. I'm thinking of lighting the BBQ and, after reading each journal, tossing them into the flames, like a funeral pyre for the person I was. As architect, contractor, builder, plumber, electrician, decorator, and landscaper on this project, I can choose to build myself up to be whatever I dare to imagine. Think it's time to buy a new journal; start   a new journey. I'd much rather focus on what is and what could be, than what was and can't be changed.   (~ heather)

Essential Information

The Chronological Journal becomes a handy and blessed reference book when you utilize those first or last two or three pages for indexing important dates and information.

Include such items as shots and immunizations for family and pets; health data like weight, blood pressure, and the start of new prescripttions or other health regimens; birthdays and anniversaries; annual dental and physical check-ups; periodic bills; furnace filter changing; automobile oil and lube; and other easily forgotten, recurring events.

In the spiral-bound menu planner and date books that I've kept, the first page of each year was left open for the recording of such dates, and the last couple of pages were held in reserve for Christmas and holiday planning and shopping lists. No one in the family ever suspected that Santa's shopping list was sitting right there on the kitchen table every year!

If you plan to use this index as a reminder, be sure to note the anniversary date ten days or so ahead of the date due. Such advance journal lists can be real sanity savers!

Many of us find that a Chronological Journal provides a solid foundation from which to expand our personal journaling endeavors. At some point you may choose to branch out and start a separate journal for dreams or other specific topics.

Chapter 13

Travel Journaling

When you travel, remember that a foreign country
is not designed to make you comfortable.
It is designed to make its own people comfortable.

— Clifton Fadiman

"Travel" seems to apply to any perambulation that takes you geographically away from home for any length of time. But whether your trip involves a tour of the mysterious back streets of Calcutta or a visit to see your grandkids in Kalamazoo, it's a fine opportunity to explore, learn, and grow. Each time you venture outside your domestic nest, you're apt to encounter the unfamiliar and sometimes the intriguing.

Travel journals or diaries have been around for a long time. Some cruise ships tuck a fresh notebook into their standard passengers' welcome packets. Write down your experiences and impressions to help set the new information in your mind. People and place names, geographical data, notes about prices and the economy in general, flavors, smells both savory and noxious, climate—if the places you visit are at all different from your home town, they represent a vast reservoir of fresh information.

When you begin a new travel journal, consider whether it will be for your eyes only or if you'll share it with others. After all, if you record your Tums purchases, the exact amounts of your tips, and other personal data, you may not be comfortable passing it around at the neighborhood show-and-tell. So decide before jotting down the first entry whether or not this will be for public consumption.

Incidentally, if your trips tend to be extensive either in time or activities, you might like to keep a separate journal for each sojourn, allowing some space for a few key photos, ticket stubs, and other memorabilia. (*See the Scrapbook Journaling chapter, p. 79, for more ideas.*)

Travel Lessons

Travel often yields unexpected changes in perspective, which in turn provide fodder for insightful journal entries such as this one:

Itaska State Park

July 17, 1987…temp 85º, sunny, no breeze 1:30 p.m.
Our first glimpse of Itaska State Park in Minnesota took our breath away. The world was suddenly filled with pine trees – magnificent pine trees, tall and stately rising above us, their lush presence replenishing our spirits with new energy. I couldn't believe such beauty.

We stopped the car and wandered down the road for a time, the sweet, pungent scent of pine perfuming the air, our voices stilled to whispers by the cathedral hush of the forest around us. Surely the secret of life itself would be revealed to us in that pristine realm of green.

Itaska is the site of the headwaters of the Mississippi River, the largest river in the United States. It starts as a thin stream of water so narrow you can walk across it without getting your feet wet. It was strange to be able to actually step across the water, which widens to nearly a mile across. In St. Louis we're used to seeing a broad "Father of Waters" and it seems inconceivable that it could ever exist as a tiny stream. (~Beverly J. Letchworth)

Here are some sample entries from a cruise journal kept by my beautiful aunt, Marguerite Waugh, on her last voyage. (She was eighty-six at the time.) They carry the tone of a seasoned traveler who is not strongly impressed with routine sightseeing:

Aunt Marg's Cruise

April 27th
(Cruise) Beautiful day!
Swam alone at 7:15. At breakfast Chas. gave me his ticket for Tangier, Morocco, on the same bus as the N_____s and Phyllis Z.

As for Tangiers's - poor people - picturesque but not enviable. Elegant homes of the rich. Very scenic, many hills & valleys. Took us through the markets (food) people sitting on the ground with their vegetables (which looked excellent) around them. Finally ended up in the rug market where they tried the hard sell. On the streets constantly pestered, importuned by sellers of all kinds. Back on ship for lunch, then to Gibraltar in the afternoon.   (~ MW)

May 15th
(Cruise) Rhodes. Swam at 7. Breakfast with Chas. Showed him yesterday's purchases - he approved (naturally!). Saw the G_____s in the Lido café and they

gave me their Wall Street Journal, which I passed along to
Annette at lunch. At tea time sat with an English family
and the Z___s. Went to the concert with Chas. and an
English couple.   (~ MW)

May 21st
(Cruise) Malaga. Breakfast with Chas. Tour of Malaga at 9
am. All high-rises - vertical concrete anthills. Distant vistas
of high-rises high on hills like visions of the future. Entire
drive very scenic. Bought a wallet ($8.50) and a tooled
leather calendar-thermometer ($6.50) and a cup of coffee
($1's worth of pesetas).   (~ MW)

A Sensory Record

Make your entries come alive by employing a generous use of
sensory words. Note the smells. Rereading your own entries about
the aromas of roasting coffee beans, rose arbors, or fish-and-sea
will instantly transport you back to a certain travel setting. Here's
an interesting technique for adding zest to your entries: pretend
you're writing as a cruise or travel director, creating sentences and
paragraphs that make the reader yearn to take the same trip.

Connor Prairie

Connor Prairie (Indiana) What a fantastic experience! This
"living history museum" is a reconstructed 1820's village
on an immense plot of land just north of Indianapolis, and
there life goes on the way it did in 1823. We could hear the
clang of the anvil as we walked down the dusty road to the
blacksmith's shop. (Any ironwork that needs to be done to
keep up the site, like making replacement door hinges, is
done at that forge.)

The weaver was in the middle of making a beautiful,
patterned red and cream wool blanket on his loom, and he

chatted with me about the trouble he had finding a certain plant that he uses for one of his dyes. He had bunches of aromatic dried herbs hanging from a rough, smoke-blackened beam near the fireplace, and claimed to be the local expert on herbal medicine. The pungent smell of drying sage and thyme scented the air in the cozy cottage.

At another house, an old, white-haired Indian fighter reminisced about being in the battle of Tippecanoe, while he sat at this table in front of the fireplace shelling black beans.

All the people who work in the village are completely immersed in 1823. If you want to talk about the next presidential election, they'll start "opinionating" about Van Buren and Harrison. Talked to one of the Connor Prairie employees while he was on lunch break – everyone who works as a docent, or guide, is required to take at least 40 hours of training—especially studying the history of the period before they can work in the village.

He also said they have the safety angle covered, with emergency phones and first aid equipment stashed in secret closets in almost every building on the property – they really are quite thorough in more ways than one!

Again, details make both the journaling and the rereading of the them a lot more interesting.

Anne Morrow Lindbergh made these journal entries during her travels with her famous husband:

Wednesday, October 4, 1933

Direct course to England. Can't get any of the English
weather stations…Southhampton: houses all in gray rows,
like caterpillars. The big calm river, with a procession of
steamers coming up from the sea.

(~ Anne Morrow Lindbergh)

Sunday, December 14, 1933

Left [in their airplane] for San Juan [Puerto Rico]. Cloudy
and heavy at Trinidad but beautiful weather all the way.
Just as I remembered it—that harebell-blue water, a little
hazy, soft, and then the green mountain islands set in
it…Hit San Juan quickly, dazzling white buildings…

(~ Anne Morrow Lindbergh)

Don't wait until your cruise ship sails or you land on the Isle of
Crete to start learning how to create a scintillating travel journal.
Practice at home. Buy an attractive journaling book, and visit your
own hometown *as though you were a tourist*. Do it in one fell
swoop, or space the observations out over a few months. One per
weekend shouldn't tax your time inordinately.

Capture the mood by taking your camera. Everything looks different when viewed though a camera lens. Make notes as you go
along, and write the entries when you return home.

This excerpt comes from a long entry about a visit to Cahokia
Mounds in southwestern Illinois, home of the (Cahokia)
Mississippian Indians (a late woodland culture), which was a
thriving metropolis from 700 A.D. to about 1500 A.D. Notice how
the written tie-in to a similar, distant archaeological site adds
dimension to the description.

Woodhenge

Excavations turned up the partial remains of at least four
and possibly five circular sun calendars of large cedar
posts evenly spaced in a 410 ft. diameter circle—called
"woodhenge" because they seem to have had the same
function as Stonehenge. These sun worshipers used them
to track ceremonial periods and season changes and
added another amazing element to their advanced
civilization—an agrarian community with real science and
engineering achievements!

Formatting Entries

Some trips lend themselves to journaling by a set format. This
ensures inclusion of all the basic information, and establishes
background for the activities and observations that follow. Travel
often combines business with pleasure, as evidenced by this entry:

Chicago - Book Expo

Date: May 31st
Weather: 84 warm & muggy
Breakfast: Cambridge House
Lunch: McCormic Center
Dinner: Szechuan East (midwest group)

Met George Smith (Gee Press) and Marg Jones (Pen
Central) at the library presentation this morning. Marg
interested in co-op marketing to independent bookstores
and self-help centers. Note: get a copy of Shel Horowitz's
Grassroots Marketing at the Expo tomorrow!

Creating a simple template for each day's entry gives you an
instant reference point on date, event, and location. Include
whatever information will prove useful to you on future review.

The Many Faces of Journaling

If you're a frequent traveler, you'll benefit from noting departure and arrival times; cost of air, train, or bus fare; gas prices, and your car's mile-per-gallon ratio; hotel and motel expenses, quality, and extra perks like continental breakfast; and any other information that could steer you either toward or away from a repeat experience.

For added interest and historical perspective, you might want to include the current monetary exchange rate and the average cost of a few basic items like a daily paper, a cup of coffee, a moderately priced dinner, or the cost per mile for a cab ride.

Some people keep a detailed list of expenses. Others put all their travel money in one pot, real or virtual, and just keep going until the supply runs dry. The latter folks often feel that paying too much attention to money takes the fun out of the experience. Use whichever system is more feasible for your situation.

If you plan to present travel/slide shows about your trip, be sure to include a full list of where, how much, when, and cautions. And ask the natives what they would suggest you include in your presentation. (You may have missed a spectacular, but less well-known site.)

Whatever methods you choose to include in your journaling, you'll wind up with rich memoirs of your travels.

Epilogue

Learning, healing, pondering, and recording through personal journaling can be a boon to healthy living. It gives you perspective into what has been and what you hope will be in your life.

Remember…that which is viewed as a burden seldom becomes a joy. Write what you want, when you want to. Approach journaling with love and humor, and leave the guilt-trips and "shoulds" behind.

I'd love to hear about your own adventures into journaling. You can e-mail me at: LindaCSenn@aol.com or write to:

Linda C. Senn
c/o Pen Central Press
P. O. Box 220369
St. Louis, Missouri 63122-0369

About the Author

Linda C. Senn, author of *The Many Faces of Journaling* 1st ed. (2001), also wrote *And Now We Dance: Journaling for the Woman Within* (2001), *Your Pocket Divorce Guide* (1999), *The Basic Divorce Workbook* (1999), and co-authored *The Divorce Recovery Journal* (1999). She's an adjunct instructor at University of Missouri/St. Louis, and gives presentations on such topics as journaling, professional writing, memoir and family history writing, and boosting your creativity. Linda helps others realize their writing goals through book coaching and ghostwriting.

She lives, writes, walks, and feeds the ducks in tree-rich Kirkwood, a suburb of St. Louis, Missouri.

෴

Bibliography

Bell, Anne Olivier, edited by. Assisted by Andrew McNeillie. *The Diary of Virginia Woolf, Volume Two*: 1920-1924. New York: Harcourt Brace Jovanovich 1978.

Frank, Otto H. and Mirjam Pressler, edited by. Translated by Susan Massotty. *Anne Frank:The Diary of a Young Girl–The Definitive Edition*. New York: Doubleday 1991.

Lindbergh, Anne Morrow. *Locked Rooms and Open Doors: Diaries and Letters of Anne Morrow Lindbergh–1933-1935.* "A Helen and Kurt Wolff Book." New York: Harcourt Brace Jovanovich 1974.

McElroy, John Harmon, edited and with an introduction by. *The Sacrificial Years: A Chronicle of Walt Whitman's Experiences in the Civil War*. Boston: David R. Godine 1999.

Perry, Bliss, edited by. *The Heart of [Ralph Waldo] Emerson's Journals*. Cambridge, MA: Houghton Mifflin/Riverside Press, 1926.

Progoff, Ira. *At a Journal Workshop: The basic text and guide for using the* Intensive Journal *process*. New York: Dialogue House Library 1975.

Sarton, May. *At Eight-Two: A Journal*. New York: W.W. Norton & Company 1996.

Senn, Linda C. *And Now We Dance: Journaling for the Woman Within*. St. Louis: Pen Central Press 2001.

The Many Faces of Journaling

Appendix A

Recommended Reading List

Bouton, Eldonna Edwards. *Loose Ends, A Journaling Tool for Tying Up the Incomplete Details of Your Life and Heart*. San Luis Obispo, CA: Whole Heart Publications, 1999.

———. *Journaling from the Heart*. San Luis Obispo, CA: Whole Heart Publications, 2000.

Cameron, Julia. *The Artist's Way Morning Pages Journal: A Companion Volume to the Artist's Way*. New York: J.P. Tarcher, 1998.

———. *The Vein of Gold: A Journey to Your Creative Heart*. New York: J.P. Tarcher 1997.

Ganim, Barbara and Susan Fox. *Visual Journaling: Going Deeper Than Words*. Wheaton IL: Quest Books, 1999.

Greene, Bob and D.G. Fulford. *To Our Children's Children: Preserving Family Histories for Generations to Come*. New York: Doubleday, 1993.

Letchworth, Beverly J. *Leaf Bird Days & Firefly Nights: Personal Renewal Through Nature Journaling*. St. Louis: Pen Central Press, 2001.

Marshall, Carl, David Marshall (contributor). *The Book of Myself: A Do-It-Yourself Autobiography in 201 Questions*. New York: Hyperion, 1997.

Neimark, Neil F., M.D. *The Handbook of Journaling: Tools for the Healing of Mind, Body & Spirit* 2nd Edition. Irvine CA: R.E.P. Technologies, 2000.

Senn, Linda C. *And Now We Dance: Journaling for the Woman Within*. St. Louis: Pen Central Press, 2001.

Senn, Linda C. and Mary Stuart, M.A. *The Divorce Recovery Journal*. St. Louis: Pen Central Press, 1999.

Slan, Joanna Campbell *Scrapbook Storytelling: Save Family Stories and Memories With Photos, Journaling and Your Own Creativity*. St. Louis: EFG, Inc.,1999.

❧

Appendix B

Create
Fascinating
Family Memoirs

A straight recital of family begats makes for a very dull memoir—
boring in both the writing and the reading. Every family has some
pizzazz tucked away here and there. Each relative has his or her
own texture and flavor, even the most ordinary of them.

Creating a family tree

An outline of family can be as formal or informal as you like. The
libraries abound with books on genealogy, which show you how to
set up a generational chart. These generally look like a down-ward
flowchart. (See example on the following page.) In the interest of
space, you may only want to list two or three generations on a
page, continuing the family line on a fresh sheet.

You may or may not want to include all the aunts-, uncles-, and
cousins-by-marriage (that is, non-blood relatives). Most likely
you'll choose to list only those who either were close to you or
seemed particularly interesting. More extensive charts are great
fodder for future genealogists, but can be a challenge to construct.

Example Family Tree

SENN FAMILY

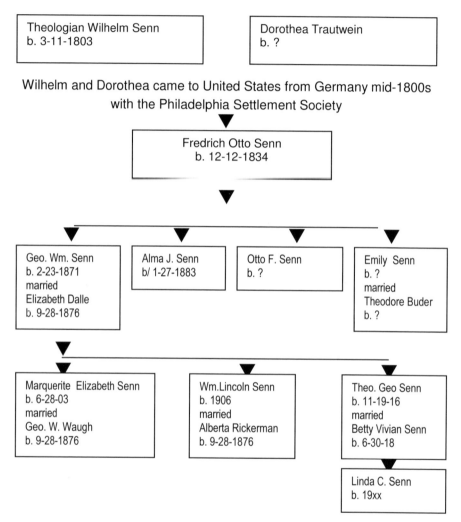

Characters

Now make a simple list of those family members on your chart and jot down something notable for each one, such as their career, artistic talent, idiosyncrasies, and/or temperament. If you knew the person, picture him or her in your mind; then write a description of physical appearance, facial expression, and a remembered event or shared activity.

For instance:

> Elizabeth Snowden Gaunt (Mannie) – my great-grandmother; short, round, laughing-twinkling blue eyes, white hair wound into a little bun with wispy fly-aways, Southern, mother of five, good cook—specialty was no-measure biscuits, loved TV wrestling, and was always piecing together a new quilt.

Mention their hobbies, even if you don't know any details: Uncle Otto was a philatelist; Mom excelled at decorative painting; Uncle Bill was the family movie photographer and banjo player; and Aunt Marg and Uncle George square-danced regularly. Be sure to note any specific life lessons you may have learned from each one.

When you write out the full family memoir, you'll have the information on your people-lists to draw from. (At this point, you may want to pass the list of people around to the family for others to add details that they remember or heard about.)

Color

Use sensory details to make people, places, and events come to life for your readers. Did your uncle smell of pipe tobacco or Old Spice? How about your grandmother? What did her kitchen smell like?

Uncle Bill laughed like a happy billy goat. Mam whistled "Lazy Bones" to get me up on sleepy summer mornings. On the other hand, my dad could produce an ear-splitting whistle by sticking his ring- and middle-fingers in his mouth. What sounds do you associate with different family members?

Include as many of the five senses—sight, smell, sound, touch, and taste—as possible. Can you describe the taste of your mother's chicken and dumplings? All of those aspects add depth and reality to your descriptions.

Chronicler

There are definite advantages to having one person act as family chronicler, to serve as the co-coordinator and central clearing-house to which family members send their written reminiscences.

Or project management may be divided among several, with one person acting as the chronicler/organizer, while another may choose to construct the family tree diagram and someone else may do the actual writing. The more people involved, the richer the content of the memoirs.

Calling all storytellers

To get the ball rolling, either by joining forces with a few others or working solo, mail out a "Call for all storytellers…" to every-one in the family. Tell them your primary objective (assembling a detailed family history) and your ultimate goal (perhaps having bound copies made for each member of the family). And be sure to set story submission and target completion deadlines. If the project is left open-ended, it'll never reach completion.

Completion

How will you know when your memoir is complete? Well, since families are essentially works-in-progress, the project may continue to grow long after the first edition has been printed and distributed. Plan the first printing about a year after the initial call for contributions goes out, and try to send a reminder or two during the year. The best of intentions can get lost in the shuffle of everyday concerns.

It's entirely possible that when people read the first edition, they'll feel stirred to send additional stories. If that proves to be the case, you can set a target of a new edition every two or five years, or whatever period seems reasonable.

Finally, when you're ready, consider having a family reunion at which to distribute this special book of memories. You can exchange written comments like the school kids do in their year-books and laugh over shared experiences.

Celebrate the love and diversity of familyhood by creating your own rich, personal history!

❦

The Many Faces of Journaling

Index

D

E

F

G

O

P

N

Q

U

V

W

Y

Z

The Many Faces of Journaling

The Many Faces of Journaling